THE KOREAN COOKBOOK

JUDY HYUN
THE KOREAN COOKBOOK

WITH AN INTRODUCTION BY
NIKA STANDEN HAZELTON

ILLUSTRATED EDITION

HOLLYM INTERNATIONAL CORP.
Elizabeth, New Jersey   Seoul

The Korean Cookbook

Copyright © 1970
by Judy Hyun

First published in 1970
by Follett Publishing Company, Chicago, U.S.A.

Copyright © 1979, 1983
by Peter Hyun

Illustrated edition, 1988
Sixth printing, 2002
by Hollym International Corp.
18 Donald Place, Elizabeth, New Jersey 07208 U.S.A.
Phone:(908)353-1655 Fax:(908)353-0255
http://www.hollym.com

Published simultaneously in Korea
by Hollym Corporation; Publishers
13-13 Kwanchol-dong, Chongno-gu, Seoul 110-111, Korea
Phone: (02)735-7551~4   Fax:(02)730-5149
http://www.hollym.co.kr

ISBN: 1-56591-001-x (Hard)
ISBN: 1-56591-002-8 (Paper)
Library of Congress Catalog Card No.: 83-81839

Printed in Korea

CONTENTS

THE KOREAN COOKBOOK

PREFACE TO THE ILLUSTRATED EDITION

Craig Claiborne, who is widely credited with pioneering serious culinary criticism in American newspapers, once remarked in The New York Times: "One of the most interesting tables in all of Manhattan is that of the Peter Hyuns. When they entertain, the food is inevitably Korean, a cuisine that seems to be increasingly popular in this country." Mr. Claiborne then persuaded my late wife to write a Korean cookbook.

The Korean Cookbook by Judy Hyun first appeared in the United States in the summer of 1970, two months before the untimely death of the author, and quickly gained the esteem of both critics and Korean food afficionados alike. A second edition was published in Seoul in 1979.

This illustrated edition of *The Korean Cookbook* owes special debts to Mr. Insoo Rhimm, the Hollym Corporation; Publishers, and his editors, who first suggested that we should reprint the book with full-color photo illustrations.

As my late wife's literary executor, I take great pleasure in dedicating this edition to the memory of the author, Judy Hyun.

Seoul
1988

Peter Hyun

INTRODUCTION
by Nika Hazelton

I first became interested in Korea at the 1964 New York World's Fair, where that country was represented by a charming pavilion and a restaurant. This restaurant turned out to be so excellent, both in food and service, that in the course of the Fair, I ate my way through the whole menu. The thing that fascinated me about Korean food— as it has all others who know it—is that it is quite different from Chinese and Japanese food. While Korean cookery is as much part of the cuisine of the Orient as French food is part of Western cooking, it nonetheless has a very individual character, and what's more, a character that appeals to the Westerner who may still have reservations about other Oriental cuisines.

As I had found Korean food so unusually delicious and interesting, I pursued it further, in order to include Korean recipes in an *Encyclopedia of Cookery* which I was compiling at the time. In seeking a Korean food expert for my entry, I met Judy Hyun and her husband, Peter. They helped me with the work, and I am happy to say that to judge from readers' reactions, the Korean entry proved to be one of the best entries on foreign food.

In getting to know the Hyuns, I found that Judy was an American girl educated in France who went to Vassar, while Peter was born in North Korea. His father, a Presbyterian minister, had died when he was a child, and his mother, a religious educator, now lives in Seoul, South Korea. Peter's education began in Korea and was continued in Paris and in the United States. It was when Peter was Cultural Attachè for the Korean Embassy in Paris, that he met Judy and married her. Before settling in the United States where they now live, Judy and Peter went to Korea, where, in the house of Peter's mother, Judy became thoroughly familiar with Korean life, and, since she liked Korean food, especially with Korean cookery. It turned out to be a wise move, because once in America, Judy discovered that her husband loved Korean food above all others—and so did her two children, Mia and Hogi, and so did her friends!

Judy's Korean home cooking was the inspiration for this book, though it has a much broader base. In order to enlarge her repertoire and be completely sure of the authenticity of her recipes and cooking techniques, Judy worked for months with Mr. Pak, the head chef of a Korean restaurant in New York City. Many are the times that I've seen them both in Judy's kitchen, measuring, chopping, slicing, stirring, seasoning and dishing up those marvelous, savory dishes, and proving that Korean food could be made without too much effort in an American kitchen. Judy's and Peter's friends were allowed to eat the results of these creative endeavors, and we all looked forward to the feasts as children do to Christmas.

Before I turn the book over to Judy, I would like to tell the reader a little about Korea. The country first became familiar to millions of Americans during the Korean War, which resulted in the tragic division of the country in 1945. Today, in North Korea, a communist system has replaced all traditional customs with new practices and values. In South Korea, where the process of modernization has been slower and the keeping or changing of traditions has been a matter of individual choice, Korean life has preserved much of its enormous charm, as is evident in many households like Peter's mother's. Since the division of Korea is an artificial one and the cookery in the two sections is about the same, it seemed unnecessary for the purposes of this book to try to divide the recipes along geographical lines.

Korea is a peninsula which borders on Siberia and Manchuria in the north, faces China to the west across the Yellow Sea and Japan to the South and east across the Korea Straits and the Sea of Japan. The size of Korea corresponds to that of approximately all of New England, New Jersey and Delaware. It is a mountainous country with thousands of lovely islands set in sparkling waters, whose climate, contrary to what one might think, is not tropical, but very much like the climate between Portsmouth, New Hampshire and Charleston, South Carolina. The natural beauty of the country is further enhanced by a wealth of monuments to Korea's ancient civilization, as different from that of the other countries of the Far East as France is different from Italy and Spain.

One of the reasons for Korea's cultural uniqueness is that the Koreans belong to an ancient race, distinct from both the Japanese and Chinese. They are thought to be the descendants of two strains, the nomadic tribes of Mongolia and the Caucasian people of Western Asia. In fact, the name of the country is thought to be derived from "Kaoli," a region of what is now Northern Manchuria. The Mongoloid tribe of Kaoli gradually moved into the northwestern part of the Korean peninsula, where they united with the existing inhabitants to make a people who were gallant horsemen, fond of feasting, dancing and poetry.

Through the centuries, Korea came under the influence of China's civilization and religions, while still preserving its individuality. For instance, the Korean spoken language is unlike Chinese, although in the same family as Japanese and Mongolian. However, for centuries, Chinese was the classical or written language up until the 15th century, when King Sejong and his scholars created a new Korean alphabet, the *hangul* or *onmun,* into which all foreign and vernacular sounds could be transcribed. Thus, although it has its own language today, one could say that Chinese is the ancient Greek of the Koreans, with which educated Koreans are familiar. Moreover, all educated Koreans now also speak and read English, which is taught in the schools.

Broadly speaking, Koreans are Buddhists, although today there are also many Christians. However, they are not religious in the Western sense of the word, and are very tolerant in their religious attitudes.

Historically, Korea paid tribute to China, although it was not politically dominated by her: there was respect and admiration on the part of the Koreans, and acceptance of non-intervention on the part of the Chinese. This changed, however, when the Japanese attempted to invade Korea in the late 16th century, and the Chinese did intervene; then about 25 years later, the Koreans attemptec to assist the Chinese when the Manchu attacked the ruling Ming dynasty. After this, Koreans were so persecuted by both the Manchu and the Japanese that the government shut the doors of the country to the outside world. So complete was her isolation that for centuries Korea became known as "The Hermit Kingdom." No foreigners were allowed to enter the country and if a Korean left, he could never return. This insulation came to an end in 1876 with the forced acceptance of a treaty with Japan, which coveted the country's rich supply of rice. Japan later annexed Korea by force in 1910.

The recent history is fresh in most Americans' minds: at the end of the second World War, Korea was divided into two occupation zones: the Russian, north of the 38th parallel, and the American south of that. The subsequent North Korean invasion of South Korea led to the Korean War in 1950, which in its turn led to the final partition of the country into North Korea and South Korea. The result is that today, North Korea is roughly the more industrialized of the two, and South Korea the more agrarian, with fishing a large part of the economy.

But now let me move from the historical to a personal view of this country, which, however war-torn and divided, remains a lovely peninsula, with quiet valleys, rugged mountains and bright waters, "The Land of Morning Calm." I will let Judy Hyun take over, and I know you will catch her enthusiasm for Korean life and food as I did, and that you, too, will want to make Korean food part of your own cooking, just as I did.

New York City
1970

A WELCOME TO "THE LAND OF MORNING CALM"

When my husband and I were married, he was the Cultural Attachè at the Korean Embassy in Paris, where we had first met. Several times a week we went to official functions, and one of my first lessons in eating Korean food was the hardest. The Ambassador gave a reception at which fried chicken was served. It was a buffet supper, and I stood, holding the plate in one hand, the thin silver chopsticks in the other, and negotiated a large chicken leg. It *is* possible to do this, and once you've mastered the technique, it's a very pleasant way to eat.

Some years and many Korean meals later, in the early sixties, we finally went to Korea. It was my first trip to the Far East and I was thrilled and excited at the prospect of seeing my husband's country and meeting his family and his many friends. Everyone we knew lived in Seoul, the capital of South Korea, and we stayed there, making the city the home-base for our travels in South Korea. North Korea of course was closed to us, since it is a country behind the Iron Curtain.

I can never forget the infinite kindness of my Korean in-laws and my husband's friends. Because of them, my view of Korea is perhaps one-sided, for the best of every household was offered to us. But then, in Korea, every guest is offered the most and the best that can possibly be afforded—and often that which can't.

From the beginning, I loved Korean food. And to answer the question that must be foremost in my readers' minds, as it once was in mine: "What is Korean food like? Is it like Chinese food or like Japanese food?" A simple but deceptive answer would be that it is like both. True enough, Korean cuisine retains many of the culinary charms of Chinese cookery, since Korea was under China's influence for so many centuries. And Japanese influence is to be found in the ingenuities of the service rather than in the food itself. But to the Korean, his cooking is as much distinguished from the Chinese or Japanese or Philippine or Indonese as to a Frenchman, his cooking is different from that of Spain, Greece, Italy or Austria.

Korean food of course has similarities with Japanese and Chinese cooking—for one, it favors rice as a staple of the diet; similar seasonings are used, but in crucially different amounts; the soybean and its byproducts are common to all. In addition, there is the critical manner of presentation: all these countries use chopsticks instead of knives and forks. The far-reaching effect of this single difference between Eastern and Western customs must not be underestimated. Chopsticks make it possible and imperative to serve food cut into small pieces, a real advantage in the Orient where there is a perennial fuel shortage. Small pieces of food need not be cooked for long and need little fuel, whereas big pieces of food, like roasts of the Western world, need a great deal of fuel for their preparation. Yet in spite of all these similarities from country to country in the East, the end result, the taste of the food, is quite dissimilar in each of them.

The Chinese, it must be admitted, are the French chefs of the Orient, the uncontested masters of a cuisine in which the variations and subtleties are infinite. While the Koreans do not have as grand a range, their cooking is no simple variation on a Chinese theme. If gross generalizations are in order, it may be said that the Chinese, again like the French, are masters of the sauce and that they also favor pork; that the Japanese eat a great deal of fish and like much of their food raw or deep fried; whereas the Koreans grill many of their foodstuffs and prefer beef.

Unlike the hot dishes of India and the peppery food of Siam, Korean cooking is discreetly spicy. Koreans mostly season their dishes with garlic, onion, red pepper, soy sauce and sesame seeds. It may be said that subtle seasoning is the key to the unique appeal of Korean food; it seems especially pleasing when compared to Japanese food, which is rather bland.

Another thing that distinguishes Korean food habits from Chinese and Japanese is that Korea has never been a tea-drinking nation. In the old days, the water in China and in Japan had to be boiled to be fit to drink. Blessed with pure water, Koreans never acquired the tea-drinking habit. Instead, there are native Korean drinks, such as ginseng, made from a perennial herb of the same name, and also local wines and spirits. More about these will be found in a later chapter.

As I said before, I took to Korean cooking at once, and tried to learn what I could about it with the help of my mother-in-law and the other female relatives. As you will see later the methods of Korean food preparation are quite different from Western ones, and I shall be forever grateful for the patience and kindness of my Korean relatives as I learned.

Once back in New York, I was to have the opportunity of learning more about Korean cooking. I met Mr. Pak, at that time head chef of the Korean restaurant Arirang, who kindly offered to show me how to make many of the marvelous dinners served there. For weeks, I watched him in his own kitchen, noting dozens of recipes and his ways of preparing them. For more weeks, Mr. Pak and I worked in my kitchen, where I cooked under his supervision. The results of my efforts were so good that the American and Korean friends whom I had called in to eat all that food urged me to write about Korean cooking. This I did, and here it is.

This book was written for all those gourmets and gourmands who like Oriental food but have never dared to make it at home, perhaps because they did not know how to prepare it or where to find the many ingredients used. I have tried to explain each recipe in detail, giving explicit instructions about ingredients. Any unfamiliar foods are fully described and I hope that their use will become as common in your kitchen as they are in mine. The recipes in this book are authentically Korean, with only a very few adaptations to American kitchen practices; I've substituted American ingredients only when the original Korean ones cannot be found in this country at all.

This book is also written for those who, familiar with

other Oriental cooking, would like to broaden their horizons and treat their taste buds to new and different pleasures. And yes, it is indeed written for Koreans, in case, by any chance, 6000 miles away from home, they have forgotten something about their native cooking.

KOREA

When I first saw South Korea, I was enchanted by its beauty. Korea is a country of rugged mountains and valleys, with a natural topography which affords its people superb vistas. The towns are surrounded by green fields of rice and majestic mountains that rise in the distance. Tiny villages dot the countryside, each one just within sight of the next. The houses of the farmers are roofed with thatch, and the thatch is covered with climbing gourds which flower in the spring and bear their fruit in the fall. Naked-bottomed babies play along the dirt road and women, clad in white, with infants tied to their backs, tread softly through the paths between the rice fields, often carrying baskets with fruits and vegetables on their heads. Old men, also clad in white, squat in front of their houses, smoking long, thin Korean pipes.

The idyllic character of much of Korea is reflected in the luxurious gardens of the country. Koreans love trees and flowers, but not the ultra-precise arrangements, the odd-shaped rocks and the stylized trees of Japanese gardens; Koreans tend to take nature as it comes and let the sunflowers sprout where they may. I found the country picturesque and gracefully vivid, with a feeling of gentle animation.

The good taste and quiet dignity of the country is evident in the costume worn by the Korean women. The basic costume consists of a long, full skirt of one color and a short jacket of another. On their feet indoors, women wear little white cloth boots, over which, when they go outside, they slip supple rubber shoes shaped like Indian canoes. These outdoor shoes are alway taken off before the women enter a house. When working, the women generally tie their skirts up at the waist, but at leisure, they pull a corner of the skirt to one side and hold it up with the hand to make walking easier.

Although there is only this one basic dress design, every dress looks different. The color combinations are unexpected and exquisite: lavender and sea green; pink and grey; all white, emphasized by a black belt and black shoes; lime green and brown; yellow, grey and old rose, complete with yellow parasol. The parasols are the high point of any ensemble: one may be a lovely mustard hue with white; another may be pink trimmed with navy lace. Imagine a whole population of ladies circulating through city or village streets on silent canoe shoes, all with billowing dresses and matching parasols!

Today even in the cities, Korean women prefer their traditional costumes to Western dress. This is not true for the men, who, except for the very old, wear Western business suits. Many elderly gentlemen still wear the traditional male Korean garment, very much like the ladies' dress, though men wear pantaloons. In the country, you may also still see the traditional Korean horsehair hat, somewhat like a piece of stovepipe set on a wide brim; the one now used, however, is smaller than the old, traditional one. All schoolchildren in Korea wear the same uniform: a white blouse with a navy blue pleated skirt for girls and a black suit with a high Chinese collar for boys.

Generally speaking, Koreans are thin and wiry people, the men more than the women, who can be plump. They are of medium height, with thick black hair and black eyes, and they look fit. A sight rare in all Korea is a *tung tung bo,* a fat man. Overweight is considered a sign of health, wealth and dignity befitting high officials, successful businessmen and rich ladies. And most definitely, Koreans do *not* look like Chinese or Japanese, but like Koreans.

The Korean house is one of the loveliest creations on earth. Usually, the houses are one storey high, and much of their charm is due to the heavy tiled roofs. Tiles, shaped like cones cut in half, were long a sign of affluence: the more tiles on your roof, the greater your prestige—which explains the fact that a Korean roof is often as large as the house itself! The roofs have an upward titlt at the corners, which gives the houses a smiling air. Interestingly, Korean houses have been heated for 1500 years with a kind of central heating, the "ondol" floor, which is paved with bricks. Under the top layer of bricks are flues which connect with a tunnel under the floor level. This tunnel carries heat from the kitchen stove throughout the house. The system, which was also known to the ancient Romans, is an amazingly efficient one, and a great comfort during the cold winter months, when the temperature in Seoul can fall below zero.

Like all Oriental homes, a Korean one is so arranged that even with only two or three rooms, the different functions of daily living can be carried out efficiently and gracefully. There is little furniture in the Western sense of the word. Since there are no beds or chairs, people sit on cushions and mats during the day and mattresses are brought out at night. Low standing tables, which are beautifully decorated with mother-of-pearl inlay on a black or red lacquer background, are hung on the walls when not in use, adding a decorative element of their own. Ink paintings and calligraphy decorate the walls; silk-embroidered screens speak of the artfulness of each housewife; and a low writing desk serves for work and study. Clothes and miscellaneous possessions are kept in ornate chests, as is the bedding. Beds are supple mattresses which are unrolled at night and spread out on the warm floor. In the morning, the mattresses are put back into the chests, to make room for daytime activities. Since so many parts of Korean life take place so close to the ground, the floors must be kept scrupulously clean.—They are.

Typical Korean houses have no dining rooms as such; a central room or a living room is used for the purpose. The most commonly used dining table is square, finished in black lacquer, which, regardless of its size, is usually ten inches high. There is also often a more elaborate dining table, hexagonal and finished in vermilion with mother-of-pearl inlays of flowers, birds or landscapes. Such a dining room table does not hang on the wall when not in use. Table cloths are not usual with any families but the wealthy.

At meal time, the dishes with the food are placed in the middle of the table, with the exception of the steamed rice, which is served in individual china bowls placed in front of each diner. A spoon with a long handle, and brass or silver chopsticks are the usual eating utensils. A knife is of course unnecessary since all the meats and vegetables are served thinly sliced.

Korean kitchen arrangements are quite different from what Americans are accustomed to. Traditionally, the stove is built-in adobe, with huge iron burners, and it burns wood, charcoal or briquets. Cooking several dishes takes time, because usually the stove has few burners. (This, incidentally, is the reason why many Korean dishes can be served either hot, warm or cold, without losing their appeal.) The brass and china kitchen utensils are generally of an artistic design and considerable diversity. Few refrigerators or ice boxes are found in traditional Korean kitchens, but fortunately, soy sauce, like salt, is a very good food preservative. (Of course, it is true that large cities like Seoul are becoming increasingly western-ized, and that more and more people, especially young ones, now live in the Western manner in Western apart-ments with the usual Western conveniences.) But in tradi-tional Korean houses, the water was carried into the

house from a pump by the multitude of servants, and
laundry was washed in the garden, in a tub, or at the
village stream. There still are many communal baths,
divided into male and female sections, as in Japan.

SEOUL

The ancient city of Seoul, capital of South Korea, lies in a
long valley and extends up the sides of the surrounding
hills. To the south it is overshadowed by the famous Nam
San Mountain, beyond which flows the Han River where
hills and cliffs run down to the blue water's edge. Seoul,
with a population of over 3 million people, is the center
of the nation's cultural, political and financial life. While
the palaces of bygone kings stand quietly hidden in their
gardens, modern architecture has built housing for the
present government.

But if the setting of Seoul is beautiful, the atmosphere
of its streets and thoroughfares is positively exhilarating.
Pedestrians, motorists and cyclists mingle in such frantic
confusion that a drive through the city is at all times an
adventure. Koreans are staunch individualists and everyone seems to feel himself master of the roadway.
Strangely, as soon as you start walking, you succumb to
the same dangerous euphoria, and saunter down the
center of side streets only to be tooted out of the way by
careening motorists. Bicycles abound, often transporting
salesmen with wares piled high above their heads. A
basket vendor, buried under a mountain of goods, ped-

dling along, is a thrilling sight. So is a restaurant delivery boy rolling swiftly along on two wheels with a tray of soup balanced on his head!

The *Myung Dong,* a section of broad streets and narrow byways in the center of the town, is closed to cars. Night and day the crowds and activity are enormous and the gaiety is catching. There are dress shops, fancy pastry shops, scores of restaurants and hotels, tearooms and stand-bars. The tearooms, in some ways comparable to French cafés, are the focal point of much social activity in Seoul, and other big cities. There are tearooms which cater to every taste: intellectual tearooms, artists' tearooms, musical tearooms, tearooms for the young and for the old. Here groups of friends discuss politics and recent books, concerts and films; mail is delivered here, messages are left, business is transacted or people just sit down and relax. For many, the tearoom is a home away from home.

The stand-bar does not enjoy the same social status. It is precisely what its name implies, a bar where you stand to drink Korean wine, beer or whiskey. These bars, which are on the rough side, have an all-male clientele; "nice girls" wouldn't be seen there.

MY EXPERIENCES WITH A KOREAN FAMILY-IN-LAW

My mother-in-law's house had one floor. There were two large rooms connected with wooden partitions. One was used as a living room, to receive guests, to eat and to sleep, and the other room served as a study. Off the entrance hall were the kitchen, the bathroom and the maids' room. The maids were country girls, glad to be in town with a nice family and a living wage, a common arrangement in Korea. In the courtyard there was a riot of flowers, tulips, azaleas and morning glories—the flowers of a temperate zone, with nothing tropical about them. My husband's family was progressive, since my father-in-law had been a Presbyterian minister in his lifetime. Although they overlooked a good deal of the stiff traditional Korean etiquette, such as constantly getting off the floor and bowing to one's mother-in-law, they were truly Korean in their overwhelming hospitality. When we came to Seoul, all the members of the family came to see us and take us around, and entertained us daily and nightly with elaborate luncheons and dinners. In the mornings, after an early "modern" breakfast of coffee and toast from an excellent German bakery, I used to go to the museums or shopping with my sisters-in-law. Both spoke fluent English and as is typical of Korea today, one wore Western dress, whereas the other stuck to her traditional Korean costume. In the afternoons, we did more of the same, went visiting or received guests. Frequently, we all took a hand at preparing the food since all the chopping and mincing that goes on before the actual cooking takes a good many hands, including those of neighbors, when a festive dinner is in the making.

If I were asked to give my impressions of traditional Korean life as I experienced it, I would say that good manners are taken for granted. Respect for one's elders, for the parents and grandparents, is part of this. The elderly are considered "superiors," and as such, total obedience is given to them by the rest of the family. No drinking, smoking, singing, loud talking or quarreling are allowed in the "superiors'" presence. They in their turn treat their juniors with affection and discretion. They can be strict, but not cruel. Korean parents play a different role in the family. The father, at least outwardly, is a stern disciplinarian. The Korean mother, on the other hand, shows the greatest tolerance for her children. Sons are more highly valued than daughters, since Korean women by convention are considered inferior to men. Thus the birth of a son is an occasion for far greater rejoicing than that of a daughter. The oldest son, as the heir to the family name, is cock of the roost, even in his childhood. He inherits most of the family property, and in return, he is expected to support the parents in their old age. If there is no son in a family, one might be adopted—often their daughter's husband, in order to preserve the family name. Korean family life is close-knit indeed, not only between parents and children, but also between brothers and sisters and their spouses. Perhaps stifling at times, it also gives a lovely feeling of warmth and belonging, a feeling that has been lost in so much American family life.

KOREAN FOOD

Koreans love to eat. A meal is the most important event of the day and much time is spent in its preparation and enjoyment. Koreans consider eating such an important function that they want to concentrate all their attention on it, and it is polite to talk as little as possible until the meal is finished. I learned this at one of the first dinner parties we went to, when I was making the usual effort to keep up a dinner table conversation that I would make at a polite Western dinner party. All I got back were fragmentary answers. After dinner, however, all was jubilant discussion. The lesson was quickly learned.

Despite the impact of the West upon Korea, the traditional Korean cuisine has not changed. When you are invited to a Korean dinner party, it will be invariably a feast. It is impolite to offer guests a small repast, so generally the hostess will spend many hours in the kitchen preparing or supervising dozens of different dishes. When everything is ready and the guests are assembled, cushions are placed on the floor around the dining table, the guests sit down and the dinner begins. But before you start to eat, the hostess bows to the traditions of Korean hospitality: she will apologize for the inadequacy of her offerings, saying that she should have made much more to do you proper honor, but that she hopes that you will enjoy what little she was able to scrape together (probably some twenty different dishes!) And away you go. A little plate the size of a demitasse saucer sits in front of you to use as a kind of dinner plate. You will have silver chopsticks and a flat silver spoon. To one side will be a bowl of soup with meat and bits of vegetables, spicy or not, depending. In the center of the table there are hot slices of raw turnip, one or two or three kinds of kimchi, and sheets of toasted seaweed. There might be spinach salad seasoned with sugar, vinegar and sesame oil; mixed vegetables such as carrots, onions, red bell peppers, zucchini and two or three different kinds of mushrooms. There will be probably a dish with transparent rice flour noodles; one or two kinds of fish, lightly sauteed in an egg-flour batter, or seasoned with soy sauce and red pepper.

When all these delicacies have been tasted, you might think the meal was at an end. But no, steaming bowls of rice are brought in from the kitchen. At an elegant dinner such as this, the guests of course must have rice, but they are not allowed to fill themselves upon a mere staple.

The main course of the meal might be *Kujol Pan,* also called *The Eight Heavenly Vegetables.* The vegetables are arranged on a large platter, in a wheel of contrasting color. In the center of the platter, there is a mound of little paper-thin rice-flour pancakes. The guest picks up one of the pancakes with his chopsticks, selects some of the heavenly vegetables, places them on the pancakes, rolls up the pancake and pops it into his mouth.

Another main course could be *The Angel's Brazier,* a mixture of meat, fish, vegetables and bean cakes over which beef broth has been poured. All this cooks and bubbles in a brass bowl suspended over a brazier filled with blazing charcoal. Of course, *Kimchi,* frequently in several varieties, is an unalterable part of any meal. And since Koreans do not eat desserts in the Western sense of the word, fruit would probably be the finish of a meal, though baked rice-molasses cakes might be served.

In other words, a Korean dinner party would more than likely consist of a bland beef soup and a highly seasoned soup, with vegetables, followed by a fish course, beef or short ribs, a pork dish and fruit. As for the serving, all the dishes would be set on the table at one time. In the old days, this was not quite so: soup, which in Korea used to come at the end rather than at the beginning of a meal, would have been brought in at the "proper" time. But now, in Korea as everywhere else, things have been simplified.

Family food is of course much simpler. The Koreans eat three hearty meals a day, all the same. Some city sophisticates may have taken to coffee and toast for breakfast, but the average family has a breakfast of soup, fish or meat, kimchi, rice and grilled fish. Lunch and dinner follow the same pattern. In the cities, husbands are apt to eat lunch in restaurants, as they do in America. School children take their lunch boxes to school. The lunch boxes are little tin boxes, with internal divisions for rice, dried fish and other food, and for the chopsticks. Small children have small chopsticks, and as the children grow bigger, so do their chopsticks. And in case you wonder, as I did, how the chopsticks are kept separate between meals and identified: each person has his own pattern and his own name engraved on his silver chopsticks, which are kept in a box when they are not being used.

Children's snacks are fruit, and occasional sweets which

can be compared to the Japanese cakes. These are made from sugar, honey, dried fruit and rice flour, and are not nearly as sweet as Western cakes or cookies.

The feasts in the Korean year which involve universal celebration are the celebration of the New Year in January, the spring festival in February, and the harvest festival in September.

Here are some random facts about Korea which surprised me. One was the absence of all dairy products: there, as in China and Japan, there is no room for a dairy industry in a densely populated country. Consequently, the fats used for cooking are vegetable fats, such as sesame oil and bean oil, made from brown beans. Another thing that struck me was the scarcity of eggs and their cost. I was not surprised that they were mostly used for decorations. I was also surprised at the number of educated women in "masculine" professions, working as doctors and lawyers as well as teachers. Uneducated women, on the other hand, don't work at all, even at the kind of jobs they would be working at in the West.

Finally, a word about Korean men in the home. However poor, no Korean man ever sets foot in the kitchen to help; he would not be caught dead there. Since the women do not seem to mind, I suppose all is well.

KOREAN RESTAURANTS

Koreans love to entertain, either at home or in restaurants. But dining in restaurants is mainly a male prerogative, and the restaurants in the evening are filled with laughing masculine voices. A Korean restaurant is often a two story structure. Downstairs there is a main dining room, the size of a large hall. Upstairs there are several private rooms. Before entering or going upstairs, the men leave their shoes at the entrance or at the bottom of the stairway. A restaurant's popularity can be easily determined by counting the number of shoes found at the door or the bottom of the stairs.

Private rooms in a restaurant—and there are many of them—are small and cozy. They have a box-like quality and they are almost invariably wallpapered with floral designs. Sitting in one gives you the feeling of being inside a gift-wrapped box: a pleasant, intimate sensation. One of the most pleasant features of the Korean restaurant meal is the Kisseng girl. Similar to the Japanese geisha, she is trained to be cultivated, charming and to look pretty. But unlike Japanese geishas, she does not wear an elaborate headdress or heavy make-up. A Kisseng girl's clothes are perhaps more sumptuous than those of ordinary Korean women, but that and her beauty are the only things that distinguish her from her domestic sisters.

At a Kisseng party, several men are seated around a low table. Between each gentleman is a Kisseng girl, smiling, arranging little delicacies on his plate, pouring wine, and offering it with all the manners of a gracious hostess. None of the girls will eat or drink anything, but they will devote all their attention to the well-being of the restaurant's guests.

KIMCHI, THE NATIONAL VEGETABLE DISH

Kimchi accompanies every Korean meal, including breakfast. This essential part of the Korean diet is a highly seasoned and fermented pickle of cabbage, turnip, cucumber and other seasonable vegetables, and it provides a large number of the vitamins in the Korean diet. Somehow, Kimchi and rice make for an excellent flavor and texture combination: the tang and the crunchiness of the first offsets the blandness and smoothness of the rice. Kimchi is also an ideal way of preserving vegetables without refrigeration, and for this reason, perhaps, Koreans grow and eat more vegetables than any other people of the Orient.

Excellent vegetables grow in the fertile Korean soil, and both fresh or à la kimchi, they are daily staples. Kimchi making is at its height in the late autumn, when all the vegetables are ripe for the making of the winter variety, the tastiest kind. In November, throughout Korea the entire female population is busy chopping and mixing the vegetables that have to last their families throughout the winter.

All over the countryside and in the city gardens, the red hot peppers are set out in large flat baskets to dry in the sun: it is a brilliant sight. Turnips, called *mo* in Korean —some as long as your arm and twice as thick—are piled high on vendors' carts pulled by husky men down country roads and city streets. When the turnips are ready, shellfish are plentiful, and the garlic crop is in. Most important,

the cabbages are ready. Korean cabbage is not the firmly
packed round head that Americans are familiar with, but
the Chinese variety, sometimes called celery-cabbage. Although there are several kinds of kimchi—in fact, as many
variations as there are households—the most common
type of kimchi is made with cabbage. The cabbages are
soaked in salted water overnight and seasoned the following day with garlic, scallions, ginger, hot pepper and anything else the cook thinks desirable. The basic recipe can
be varied by adding radishes, anchovy paste, shrimp or
oysters, bits of meat and whatever is at hand. In any event,
no two kimchis ever turn out the same. When the mixture
has been mixed and packed away in the huge earthen jars
in which it is to ripen, the housewife can only hope for
the best and pray that the lot will be good and last
through the winter.

Kimchi jars are of the Ali-baba-and-the-forty-thieves
variety, and each is capable of holding a man. These jars
are stored underground, in a hole in the backyard, or in a
special storeroom built in the earth for this purpose,
something resembling the potato houses in potato fields
where tubers are stored. Many households in large cities
have such kimchi houses; and for apartment dwellers,
there are communal backyards especially for the storing
of the kimchi jars. A heavy weight, such as a stone, must
be placed on the lid of the clay jars, because when the
kimchi starts to ferment after a few weeks, the water
drawn by the vegetables literally boils. Kimchi must ferment in peace and quiet for at least a month. It is at its

best after two or three months, and it will keep for a year
without changing its basic taste.

RICE

The closest Korean equivalent to Western bread is rice.
Legend has it that rice originated in Ha-Ram, China,
somewhere between 2838 BC and 2698 BC; this means
that from being a wild grass, it became sufficiently do-
mesticated to cultivate. Rice was introduced into Korea
in 1122 BC by a Chinese nobleman. In Chinese, rice is
called *syang-non-si,* which means "marvelous architecture," and it is as vital to the Korean style of life as it is to
the Chinese.

The two chief varities of rice grown in Korea are ordinary paddy-field rice, called *tap-kik,* which is used for
everyday boiling and eating, and the other is upland rice,
which is usually dried and used for making rice flour and
for brewing beer. Since rice is Korea's basic starch, it is
eaten at every meal, from breakfast on. It is served in
many ways. Mashed with chestnuts, it is fed to babies as
we would feed them baby cereals; it is milled into flour
and made into a variety of cakes with mashed red beans
or fruits and nuts; or it may be mixed with other grains
and vegetables to stretch or vary the menu. Most often
rice is boiled, though it may also be steamed or fried.

The Koreans, following general Oriental practice, always cook rice in just enough water so that by the time
the water has evaporated, the rice will be tender. Since

the water is never drained off, none of the nutrients in the rice are wasted. In fact, it is thought that the richest part of a pot of rice is at the bottom. Rather than waste any grains that may stick to the pan, a cup or two of water is added after the cooking. This water simmers slowly during the meal. Afterwards the "rice water" is drunk much as Americans drink an after-dinner cup of coffee.

Americans feel that they have made a successful rice dish if each grain is dry and separate; the Koreans, on the other hand, favor grains which are wet and sticky, with a mushy taste. The texture of the rice is determined by two factors: the type of rice and the age of the grains. Long grain rice seems to be most popular in America, whereas a more rounded grain, which becomes much softer in cooking, is preferred by the Koreans. Secondly, new rice is quite different from rice that has been stored for some time: it has a fresher taste and is whiter in color.

Rice is also sometimes added to other grains. When I was in Korea in October, I saw that almost all the rice was mixed with barley. We were at the end of the old season and the new rice crop had not yet been harvested. What supplies remained had to be stretched. But when toward the end of the month, the first new rice became available, the difference in taste and texture was noticeable indeed.

OTHER GRAINS

Millet, the only grain native to all Korea, is sometimes used as a substitute for rice. In North Korea it is also used in certain concoctions such as *Sikhe,* which, believe it or not, is made of salty fermented fish (head, bones and all), turnips and millet.

Wheat and barley are also grown in Korea, but no grain enjoys the same venerable reputation as rice.

DRIED INGREDIENTS

Dried vegetables and roots are also used in Korean cooking. One of these is *Toraji,* the root of the bellflower; and another is a brown fern which resembles a rather resilient brown noodle.

Dried beans are used as additives. The most famous bean is of course the soy bean, world-renowned for its highly nutritious qualities. A number of products essential to the Korean diet are made with it: soy sauce, soybean pastes, bean sprouts, bean curd and soy milk. The latter two are the "dairy products" of Korea.

GINSENG

Probably the most famous and unique product of Korea is *ginseng,* a root shaped like the human body. Ginseng was prized for centuries throughout the Far East and at the Russian and French courts as well, for its aphrodisiac and rejuvenating qualities. Today, ginseng is still used in Korea, Japan and elsewhere in the Orient for this aphrodisiac effect. It is also said to be beneficial in curing a number of illnesses. Supposedly good for everyone's health, regardless of age and sex, ginseng is particularly known for its advantageous effect on the health of older gentlemen, its principal devotees.

The word "ginseng" comes from two Chinese words, meaning "man" and "plant." The larger the plant, and the more it resembles the human form, the more valuable it is. Wild ginseng was once worth its weight in gold, and the mountains in the north of the country were thoroughly scoured in an effort to discover it. Such generous rewards were offered for this valuable root (an extraordinarily fine specimen was worth $2000) that many men would spend months at a time searching for it. "But," said an English traveler in 1887, "the magic properties which the herb is reported to possess prevent its discovery except by those who lead a pure life, and the market has consequently never yet been over-stocked." Needless to say, ginseng has been cultivated commercially for a long time, particularly in the west-central provinces of Hoang-Hai Do (now in North Korea) and Kyon-Kwi Do (near Seoul).

Commercial ginseng is made into a variety of products. There is ginseng tea, ginseng liqueur, made from barley alcohol with a large piece of ginseng in the bottle, and instant ginseng, which looks like a lighter instant coffee. Ginseng liqueur is for the gentlemen, and ladies, who don't drink strong spirits in Korea, sip their ginseng as tea.

Ginseng excites the nervous system, and several American friends who have become ginseng enthusiasts declare that there is a marked effect if the root is taken regularly for a few weeks. Reportedly, it tastes like medicine at the first try, becomes palatable at the second, and those who get to the third drink become lifelong ginseng drinkers. It is, like coffee, an acquired taste, but one that is thought delicious by its devotees.

FRUIT

The fruit of Korea is beautiful. There are apples, peaches, strawberries, pears, watermelon, blackberries, pomegranates, currants, cherries—all exquisite. I remember especially the large, red, juicy, firm apples, the fragrant peaches and the pears best of all, for they are juicy and crunchy, as no American pears are; even when perfectly ripe, they still retain a refreshing firmness.

Fruit is served to visitors morning and afternoon and with each meal. It comes to the table peeled and cut into bite-size pieces ready to pop into the mouth. It is a perfect conclusion for a spicy Korean meal.—Unfortunately, the meal has often been so copious that hardly any room is left for these delicious fruits!

SWEETS AND DESSERTS

Although cakes and pastries are not usually served with meals, many small shops specialize in such goodies. There are spongy, rich cakes, much like our angel food cakes in their bouncy texture, chestnut balls, pounded date balls and many other confections often filled with a red-bean paste which takes the place of our pastry cream fillings.

SEAFOODS

Korea is a country surrounded on three sides by water, so products of the sea abound. There are at least seventy-five varieties of fish and twenty different kinds of shellfish. There are shrimp, mackerel, Alaska pollock, anchovies, hairtails, flatfish, whiting, sole, flounder, cod, herring and smelts. Carp and salmon live in the numerous streams, where fresh water fish are cultivated commercially. Oysters are also cultivated, as are lavers, a special kind of seaweed which grows around poles planted on the shores of the sea. Several other kinds of seaweed are gathered and highly prized for their nutritive value: seaweed soup is a must for expectant mothers. Every conceivable kind of fish and even some inconceivable ones are greatly appreciated and served, either raw, freshly steamed or salted and dried. Packages of dried fish the size of a pin can be bought at all markets. Along the docks, endless yards of fish can be seen drying in the sun; later, the fish are packed into large wooden barrels. Cuttlefish are strung up on lines, and blow in the wind like so many flags decorating a fairground. It is an amazing sight—and an amazing smell.

The importance of fish in the Korean diet can be appreciated when you realize that according to the latest statistics of the Korean government, 85% of the nation's animal protein intake comes from fish.

BEVERAGES

As I said before, Koreans do not drink tea the way the Chinese and Japanese do. The beverage which usually accompanies a Korean meal is barley water. Toasted barley, boiled for a few minutes, gives a faint but agreeable flavor to the water; it is drunk cold in summer and warm in winter. And at the end of a meal, hot rice water is often served, as I mentioned earlier.

The native alcoholic drink is the rather weak *yakju*, which is brewed from rice. It is a creamy liquid, acidulous in flavor, like a mixture of white wine and yogurt. *Soju* is a strong spirit distilled from wheat, clear like vodka. Often fruits and flowers are added to the *soju* to make flowery infusions like *igangju* (plum ginger wine), *omiju* (magnolia wine) *paekhwaju* (hundred flower wine) and *kukhwaju* (chrysanthemum wine). All these flowery liquors are on the dry side and are much relished by gentry. Incidentally, the *ju* in these words means wine, and since every alcohol, including spirits, is called "wine" in Korean, these "flower wines" are really flower spirits.

Koreans also make excellent beer, from barley. The beer is of the lager variety, and it was originally introduced by German brewers.

SOME COMPARISONS

Some foods taken for granted by Americans are hardly ever seen in Korea. As I said before, there is no dairy industry, ahd the always scarce milk is for the very young only; it is for this reason that babies are often weaned as late as two years. With no milk, milk-based dishes such as custards, cream sauces, puddings and creams are un-heard-of. Butter is also a rarity.

As for cheese, I have yet to meet a Korean who could truthfully say that he loved cheese. "Our kimchi pickles smell like sweet perfume compared to well-aged cheese" Koreans will say.

Noodles are great favorites. Most frequently, they are made from rice flour. A common sight in Korean back-yards is homemade noodles strung on clotheslines to dry out.

SHOPPING FOR A KOREAN DINNER

Glance through the recipes and decide which ones are suitable for the occasion you have in mind. There are a number of meat and casserole dishes, which, combined with steamed rice, would make a simple meal along west-ern lines. Or, if you are going to serve a real Korean meal with several different kinds of meat, fish and pickles, look at the suggested menus. In any event, make a list of the ingredients needed for each dish you plan to serve; you may have to take a trip to your Oriental grocery.

When you are buying fresh vegetables, remember that

the authentic taste of the finished dish is in direct proportion to the freshness of the vegetables. Always try to buy vegetables that have been trimmed the least.

A garden-fresh pepper will keep in the refrigerator for several weeks before it starts to wrinkle—so gauge the age of wrinkled-looking peppers you see on the market: it may be considerable. The same applies to eggplant and zucchini. Scallions may also be kept for weeks by merely peeling off the outer skins and trimming the wilted edges. In the store, though, look for untrimmed scallions, which will be far more flavorful than old wilted ones, making a crucial taste difference in your recipe.

Most meats in Korean cooking must be thinly sliced so that they will cook quickly. Tough cuts will not do for meats which are to be grilled. Flank steak is good for grilling, because it is easy to cut and it may also be halved and frozen for another time. But sirloin is even better, and if you want to use filet mignon, it is better still.

Remember that the requisite spices and flavorings are the key to a Korean meal. Dried ingredients like seaweed will keep indefinitely, but spices do not, and they should be replaced when they begin to lose their flavor.

PREPARING YOUR KOREAN DINNER

The main job in preparing the meal will be the chopping and/or slicing. When everything is chopped or sliced, there is little else to do. Experienced Korean cooks slice and chop so quickly that the procedure seems like child's play. It is not, though, and here are a few tips:

1. Buy a large chef's knife and a knife sharpener, and use them constantly.
2. The slicing of the meats and vegetables is extremely important. There are three different techniques: the *straight cut,* the *diagonal cut* and the *turning cut.*

Straight cut: Take, for instance, a cucumber. If the recipe calls for slices of cucumber 2 inches long, divide the whole cucumber into 2-inch lengths. Then slice these lengths lengthwise. You will have flat rectangles of cucumber rather than round slices, which Koreans seldom if ever use.

Diagonal cut: It is used extensively, especially for meats. This technique is like cutting on the bias. For example: If a 1-inch-thick steak is to be cut on the diagonal, slant the knife at a 45-degree angle and slice down through the meat with a left to right motion (if you are right-handed). This cut will produce a slice of meat which is much wider than the actual 1-inch steak. This kind of slicing cuts across the fibers, which allows the meat to cook more quickly and yet remain tender. Diagonal cutting in vegetables, especially long, round ones, produces an oval or elliptical slice.

Turning cut: It is used a great deal in making pickles and slicing large vegetables such as Chinese turnips. This is actually a straight cut except that the vegetable is turned as the cutting progresses. Take a carrot, slice it a few times lengthwise, roll it over so that it rests on what is now a flat side. This rolling is more a convenience in cutting than a technique. It helps keep the vegetable from slipping and exposes the largest surface at the top for you to grasp.

POSITION OF THE KNIFE

Hold the food with your left hand, thumb underneath and four fingers on top. Hold the knife with your right hand. Push the food towards the knife. Keep the tip of the knife on the cutting board, but raise the handle and bring it down on the food to be sliced. In other words, the knife is kept stationary, and the food is moved along as it is being sliced.

SCORING

Korean grilled meats are often marinated in various seasonings before cooking. Scoring, which is the process of cutting lines into the meat, allows the marinade to penetrate further into the meat and shortens cooking time. Sometimes, the scoring is light, as for fish or shrimp. Sometimes, as in heavy cuts of beef, the scoring is very deep, down to the bone. Scoring also prevents some cuts from shrivelling or curling when cooked over a high heat or in hot oil.

CHARCOAL GRILLING

Charcoal-grilled dishes are one of the distinctive features of Korean cooking, as has been mentioned. Of course this fits easily into the American backyard way of life. The distinctive Korean flavorings, though, add a delightful variety to barbecue evenings. Friends of mine gave a large buffet for two hundred people and served *Bul-Gogi* with toothpicks; the experiment was a terrific success. Every guest was pleasantly amazed at the flavor of this Korean specialty, and there were no regrets for the prosaic old standbys, cold ham and turkey. The only qualification to a standard American backyard grill is that you must have one with small openings, so that the small pieces of food will not drop through onto the coals.

COOKING TIME

Assemble all the ingredients for your Korean meal and prepare them according to recipe instructions. Then you are ready to begin the actual cooking. This is often a last-minute operation. However, you will want to wash and soak the rice an hour before you plan to eat. Actual cooking time for the rice will only take about 20 minutes.

One factor which determines cooking time is the way in which the food has been cut. The smaller the pieces and the more exposed surfaces, the faster food will cook. Freshness is another variable. The fresher the vegetable, the faster it will cook. Finally, do not forget that the cut and consequent toughness of meat plays an important part in determining cooking time.

One recommendation that applies to all styles of cooking, not just Korean cooking, is not to overcook your fish. Unlike meat, fish is 65 to 80% moisture. Fish is done when it reaches an internal temperature of 145°; after which every second in the pan means fibers toughened, juices and flavor lost. If the fish can be flaked at all, it is done. It does not have to flake easily. The reason why many Americans are reluctant to eat fish is that they have always been served overcooked fish. Hence the stringy texture, the "fishy" smell and taste. The Japanese eat raw fish, which has no "fish odor" at all.

Koreans like their vegetables slightly crunchy, as do the Chinese. Vegetables taste better when they have not been boiled down to a mush, as most Americans will discover.

SERVING YOUR KOREAN DINNER

If you are living in America, you may want to take off your shoes, sit down on the floor, perhaps around your coffee table and eat pickled cabbage with chopsticks. On the other hand, you may find that this is carrying authenticity too far. There are, however, a number of more conventional ways of enjoying the delicious flavor of Korean food. In this book, there are a number of "main dish" meat and vegetable dishes. If you wish to entertain, there are several spectacular Korean dishes which are not really difficult or too time-consuming. If you wish to entertain buffet style, there are several dishes that may be prepared in advance and eaten warm, lukewarm or even cold. Or if you want to serve a real Korean dinner, with as many as a dozen different dishes, you will need half a day to prepare all the recipes.

At the bottom of many recipes there is the notation: "Makes 2 to 6 servings." This means that if it is used as a main dish, it will not serve more than two. But if you are serving two, three or more additional dishes, Korean-style, there will be enough for 4 and even for 6. You, of course, are the best judge of your guests' appetites.

Do remember that Korean food is prepared with chopsticks in mind. If you can, use them; if you cannot, *try*.

Knives are considered barbaric instruments appropriate only for kitchen use. Clearly, if food is not to be cut at the table, it must be either so soft that it will fall apart, as chicken and fish should, or else, it should be cut into pieces small enough to be manipulated with chopsticks.

How to use chopsticks: hold your hand horizontally parallel to the table, palm facing you. Rest the chopsticks across the top of your middle finger. Place your thumb across the top of the chopsticks to hold them down firmly. With your thumb still in position, roll the chopstick furthest from you toward your index finger, then roll it back tightly into position with your index finger. Practice this rolling movement a few times, and you will soon be able to negotiate things which are not too slippery, and master slippery ones with practice.

Incidentally, you will notice that Korean-style rice is one of the easiest things to pick up with chopsticks, because it sticks to them! It's all part of a master plan!

SOUPS

BAIK SUK
WHOLE SPRING CHICKEN SOUP

Korean soups may be thick and hot or clear and delicate,
spicy or bland. A soup generally accompanies every meal,
and some, like the soup below, may be a meal in itself.
Accompanied by a little boiled rice and perhaps a hot
pickle, Baik Suk is a nourishing but light supper. In Korea, it
is thought to be especially good for recuperating invalids.

4 1½-pound spring	4 scallions
chickens	salt
4 cups water	pepper

1. Place the 4 chickens in a pot, cover with the water and
bring to a boil. Skim off the froth and cover the pot.
Reduce the heat and simmer for 30 minutes.

2. Serve each chicken with its juice in individual soup
plates. Mince the scallions and use as seasoning along with
salt and pepper.

Makes 4 servings.

YOUNG KAE BAIK SUK
SPRING CHICKEN SOUP

1 1½-pound spring chicken	1 tablespoon salt
3 cloves garlic	1 teaspoon soy sauce
2 scallions	dash black pepper
2 teaspoons sesame oil	4 cups water

1. Chop the chicken into 1½-inch lengths. Slice the garlic thin and cut the scallions into 1½-inch lengths.

2. Heat the sesame oil in a heavy-bottomed pot. Brown the chicken pieces, garlic, scallions, salt and soy sauce for about 5 minutes or until the chicken is golden brown. Add the water and bring to a boil. Season with black pepper. Skim off the froth, cover and let the soup simmer for 30 minutes.

Makes 4 servings.

MALGUN KUK
CLEAR BEEF BROTH

If a dish calls for beef stock and there is none available, this recipe may be used as an instant substitute.

½ pound ground beef   5 cups water
2 tablespoons cooking oil

1. While browning the meat in a heavy pot for 5 minutes over a high flame, separate the chunks.

2. Add the water and bring to a boil. Skim off the froth. Cook for 15 minutes, then strain.

Makes 4 cups.

SOKKORI KUK
OXTAIL SOUP

The oxtail is the most flavorful piece of meat you can buy:
it imparts a flavor quite distinct from other cuts of beef
to any soup.

1 oxtail (in pieces)	1 carrot
6½ cups water	3 cloves garlic
1 medium onion	1½ teaspoons salt
5 scallions	

1. Brown the oxtail in a heavy pot, add the water and bring
to a boil slowly. Skim off the froth. Halve the onion and
2 of the scallions. Add them to the oxtail. Cover and
simmer for 3 hours.

2. Slice the carrot lengthwise into 1½-inch strips. Chop
the garlic and the 3 remaining scallions. Add the carrot,
garlic and scallions to the soup. Season with salt.

Makes 4 servings.

SOKKORI GOMTANG
OXTAIL AND BEEF SOUP STOCK

This recipe makes a delicious soup stock from which a
variety of other soups can be made. The beef may be used
in a number of ways: served sliced with aspic, cooked
in beef soup or marinated in soy sauce.

1½-pounds beef shin	1 large onion
1 oxtail	3 scallions
10 cups water	

1. Cut the beef shin into 2 large pieces. Request the bone
if the butcher has it. Have the oxtail cut into 8 or 10 pieces.

2. Brown the meat and bone in a heavy pot. Add the
water and bring slowly to a boil, skimming off all the froth.
Simmer, covered, for 2 hours. Remove the beef shin. Halve
the onion and scallions and add them to the pot. Simmer
for an additional hour. Strain.

Makes 6 to 8 cups.

MANDU KUK
"RAVIOLI" SOUP

"Ravioli" soup is a cool weather specialty, usually served at Chinese New Year (around February 1st) or on some family occasion such as birthdays. Different sections of the country make this soup in various ways: north of Seoul, tiny dumplings are enveloped with a large thin sheet of dough and boiled underneath this cover, which must be broken when the soup is eaten. There are also square-shaped raviolis, crescent-shaped and triangular-shaped dumplings, each the specialties of different cooks.
The crescent-shaped one is particularly difficult to master. However, this recipe is not as complicated as it may appear at first glance. Dumpling skins may be purchased at an Oriental grocery store; a package will serve six people.

The Dough
1½ cups sifted flour   ½ cup water

1. Make a well in the center of the flour. Slowly add about ½ cup of water, mixing well by hand. Knead the dough; it should be a little stiff. Cut the dough in half, then roll out each half as thin as possible with a floured rolling pin. Cut out circles with a water glass; for additional thinness roll each circle again. There should be 30 to 35 skins. If using prepared skins, quarter the entire package.

The Filling

1 cup ground meat	1 cake bean curd
½ pound or 3 cups bean sprouts	1 tablespoon sesame oil
2 leaves Chinese cabbage	1 teaspoon sesame seeds
1 medium onion	½ teaspoon salt
1 scallion	1 egg
2 cloves garlic	pepper

1. Wash and then steam the bean sprouts for 5 minutes. Mince the Chinese cabbage, onion, scallion and garlic. Chop the bean sprouts coarsely and combine them with the bean cake in a cheesecloth or clean dish towel. To avoid a watery filling, squeeze out as much water as possible. Place the sprouts and bean cake in a mixing bowl and add all the other ingredients. Mix well by hand.

2. Beat the egg. Using a fingertip, moisten 2 sides or one-half the circumference of the dough with the beaten egg. Place a teaspoonful of the meat mixture on each round of dough, fold over the round, and pinch the edges together tight. During cooking, the egg will harden and seal the edges together.

Variations: Use any combination: ½ beef with ½ pork; ½ beef with ½ chicken; or all beef.

The Soup

4 cups beef stock	2 teaspoons salt
2 scallions	1 egg, slightly beaten
¼ cup soy sauce	

1. Heat the stock to boiling. Cut the scallions into 2½-inch lengths and add them to the stock with the soy sauce, salt. Drop the ravioli into the soup and boil for 5 minutes, covered. Add the egg, stir and serve.

Variations: Instead of boiling the ravioli in soup, they may be steamed and served separately with a soy sauce dip. The ravioli taste delicious fried in a small amount of sesame oil. If the ravioli brown on the outside before the filling has had a chance to cook through, lower the heat and cover the pan for a few minutes. Fried ravioli may also be served with a soy sauce dip.

DOMI CHIGAE
HOT RED SNAPPER SOUP

A chigae is usually a hot soup comprised of several ingredients. In this case, meat has been cooked with fish—the one to impart body, the other to add flavor.

¼ pound lean beef
   (shoulder)
1 1½ to 2-pound red
   snapper
2 scallions

2 cloves garlic
½ cake bean curd
2 cups water
2 tablespoons kochu
   chang (See page 263)

1. Shred the beef into 2-inch lengths. Cut the red snapper across the body into 1½-inch widths, leaving the bones inside. Cut the scallions into 2-inch lengths and slice the garlic thin. Cut the bean cake into 1-inch cubes.

2. Arrange the pieces of fish on the bottom of a pot. Add the scallions, then the beef. Now add the garlic. Mix the kochu chang with water and pour it over the other ingredients. Bring to a boil, then reduce the heat and simmer for 20 minutes. Just before serving add the bean curd and cook for 2 minutes.

Makes 4 servings.

Variation: Instead of red snapper, use a 1½ to 2-pound sea bass, or a 1-pound codfish, or 2 small lobsters.

SAIWU CHIGAE
HOT SHRIMP SOUP

4 shrimp
½ pound fish fillet
1 medium-sized onion
2 scallions
2 Chinese mushrooms
4 button mushrooms

½ leaf Chinese cabbage
1 cake bean curd
2 cups beef stock
2 tablespoons kochu
    chang (See page 263)

1. De-vein the shrimp. Cut the fish fillet into 2-inch pieces. Cut the onion into slivers, halve the scallions lengthwise and then cut them into 2-inch lengths. Soak the Chinese mushrooms for 30 minutes, then quarter them. Halve the button mushrooms. Slice the chinese cabbage into 1½-inch squares. Cut the bean cake into 6 pieces.

2. Put all the ingredients into a soup pot. Add the stock and bring to a boil. Season with the kochu chang and simmer, covered, for 10 minutes.

Makes 2 to 4 servings.

Variation: Add 2 cloves of sliced garlic to the soup ingredients.

MALGUN KAJAE KUK
CLEAR LOBSTER SOUP

Clear soups are those in which the ingredients are boiled in water. Rich soups are made by browning the meat or fish in oil first.

¼ pound lean beef (shoulder or flank)	1 clove garlic
	4 cups water
4 scallions	1 teaspoon soy sauce
1 medium-sized lobster	1 tablespoon salt

1. Slice the beef thin, then cut it into 1-inch squares. Cut the scallions into 1-inch lengths. Wash the lobster, then chop (or have a fish dealer chop it) into 1½ inch pieces at the joints. Mince the garlic.

2. Bring the water to a boil. Add the beef and lobster pieces and bring this mixture to a second boil. Skim off the froth. Add the scallions, garlic, soy sauce and salt. Cover the pot, lower the flame and simmer for 30 minutes.

Makes 4 servings.

Variation: For a rich lobster soup, follow the procedure for rich soups. Brown the beef, lobster, scallions, garlic and salt in 1 tablespoon sesame oil. Add the water and soy sauce. Cook, covered, for 30 minutes.

DAEHAP KUK
CLAM SOUP

1 pound ground beef or
   thin beef slices
⅛ of a pound Chinese
   turnip or ½ cup, sliced
2 scallions
½ teaspoon sesame oil
¼ teaspoon salt
dash pepper
¼ pound mushrooms
¼ teaspoon salt

dash pepper
1 tablespoon flour
3 clams
salt
pepper
1 teaspoon flour
1 tablespoon cooking oil
2 eggs
3 cups chicken broth

1. Slice the beef into matchstick-shaped pieces. Slice the turnip into rounds, then into matchstick-shaped pieces. Cut the scallions into 2-inch lengths. Mix the meat, turnip and scallions with the sesame oil, salt and pepper.

2. Remove the stems from the mushrooms and sprinkle the caps with salt, pepper and flour. Mix well.

3. Scrub the outside surface of the clam shells thoroughly. Open the clams and reserve the shells. Sprinkle the clams with salt, pepper and flour.

4. Heat 1 teaspoon cooking oil in a heavy skillet. Beat the eggs slightly, in a bowl. Dip the mushroom caps into the eggs, then fry until golden-brown on both sides. Remove the caps from the pan. Add more oil to the pan

Ravioli Soup (*Mandu Kuk,* see p. 48)

Oyster Soup (*Kul   Kuk*, see p. 58)

Rich Seaweed Soup (*Ginchang Kuk*, see p. 62)

Yellow Bean Sprout Soup (*Kong Namul Kuk*, see p. 63)

Skewered Beef (*Sogogi Sanjuk,* see p. 86)

Short Ribs in Sweet Sauce (*Kalbi Kui,* see p. 91)

Barbecued Beef (*Bul Kogi*, see p. 85)

Boiled Beef in Sauce(*Sogogi Pyunyuk,* see p. 103)

Raw Meat(*Yuk Whe,* see p. 111)

Beef Marinated in Soy Sauce (*Sogogi Chang Chorim*, see p. 110)

Liver Sauteed in Egg Batter (*Gan Chunyua*, see p. 128)

Fish Saute (*Saengsun Buchim,* see p. 144)

Seaweed: Thin Laver (*Kim,* see p. 169)

as needed. Dip the clams into the eggs and fry for 1 minute. Pour the remaining eggs over the clams to make a clam omelet. Fry until golden on both sides. Remove the omelet from the pan.

5. On the bottom of a soup pot arrange the meat, turnip and scallion mixture. On top of this mixture, place 3 clamshells, then the mushrooms. Put the clam omelet over all the ingredients. Add 3 cups chicken broth and heat to boiling. Do not stir. Skim off the froth and simmer for 10 minutes to blend the flavors.

Makes 2 to 4 servings.

Variations: Substitute a chicken bouillon cube and clam juice for the chicken stock.
Substitute oysters for the clams.

DAEHAP DAENCHANG KUK
CLAM SOUP WITH BROWN SAUCE

¼ pound lean beef
  (shoulder, chuck or
  flank)
1 cup cut fresh spinach

3 scallions
16 clams
¼ cup daenchang
4 cups beef stock

1. Slice the beef thin, then cut it into 1-inch squares.
Cut the spinach into 1-inch squares and the scallions
into 1-inch lengths. Open the clams, reserving the
liquor, if possible.

2. Mix the daenchang and the stock in a cooking pot.
Add the beef and bring the mixture to a boil. Skim off the
froth. Add the clams and any liquid from them as
well as the spinach and scallions. Continue cooking
for 5 minutes.

Makes 4 servings.

Variation: For a rich clam soup, follow the procedure for
rich soups. Shred the beef, open the clams and cut
the spinach and scallions. Heat 1 tablespoon sesame oil
in a pot. Brown the meat, then the scallions. Brown the
spinach and clams briefly. Add the stock and daenchang.
Frozen spinach may be used. It should be cut into
1-inch squares. One cup is needed.

KUL DAENCHANG KUK
OYSTER SOUP WITH BROWN SAUCE

¼ pound lean beef
   (shoulder or flank)
12 oysters

1 cup cut Chinese turnip
¼ cup daenchang
4 cups beef stock

1. Shred the beef into 2-inch lengths and shell the oysters, reserving the liquid, if possible. Cut the turnip into ½-inch cubes.

2. Mix the daenchang and the stock in a cooking pot. Add the beef and bring to a boil. First skim off the froth. Add any liquid from the oysters. Add the turnip and continue cooking for 35 minutes. Add the oysters and cook for 5 minutes longer.

Makes 4 servings.

Variation: For a rich turnip-oyster soup, follow the procedure for rich soups. Shred the beef, open the oysters and cut the turnip. Heat 1 tablespoon sesame oil in a pot, then brown the meat. Brown the turnip and oysters for a few seconds. Add the stock and daenchang.

KUL KUK
OYSTER SOUP

¼ pound lean beef   12 oysters
  (shoulder, chuck or   1 tablespoon sesame oil
  sirloin)   1 teaspoon soy sauce
1 scallion   1 tablespoon salt
1 clove garlic   4 cups beef stock or water
1 cup shredded Chinese
  turnip

1. Shred the beef into 2-inch lengths. Cut the scallion
into 2-inch lengths and crush the garlic. Shred the turnip
into 2-inch lengths. Open the oysters, reserving
as much of the liquid as possible.

2. Heat the sesame oil in a heavy-bottomed pot. Brown
the meat. Add the scallion, garlic, turnip, soy sauce and
salt. Stir-fry for 30 seconds. Add the stock or water
and bring to a boil. Reduce the heat and place a tight-
fitting lid on the pot. Cook for 25 minutes. Add the
oysters and the liquid. Cook for 5 minutes longer.

Makes 4 servings.

CHOGAE DAENCHANG DUBU KUK
MUSSEL AND BEAN CURD SOUP

½ pound tender beef
1 clove garlic
1 scallion
24 mussels

2 cakes bean curd
1 tablespoon sesame oil
4 cups beef stock
1 teaspoon salt

1. Slice the beef into thin strips. Slice the garlic and scallion. Scrub the mussels carefully to remove all the sand. Slice each bean cake into 6 pieces.

2. Heat the oil in a pot, brown the beef quickly and add the garlic and scallion. Stir-fry for 30 seconds, then add the stock. Bring the mixture to a boil, add the bean cakes and mussels. Skim off the froth and cook for 5 minutes or until mussel shells open. Season with salt to taste.

Makes 4 servings.

MYUNGTAE DAENCHANG KUK
WHITING SOUP WITH BROWN SAUCE

½ pound lean beef
  (shoulder, chuck or
  flank)
1 pound whiting
1 scallion

2 cloves garlic
½ cake bean curd
¼ cup daenchang
4 cups beef stock

1. Shred the beef into 2-inch lengths. Cut the whiting
into 2-inch lengths, leaving the bones inside. Cut the
scallion into 2-inch lengths. Slice the garlic thin and then
slice the bean cake.

2. Mix the daenchang and stock in a cooking pot. Add
the beef and whiting. Bring the mixture to a boil, then
skim off the froth. Add the scallion and garlic and cook
for 10 minutes. Just before serving, add the bean cake
slices and cook for 2 minutes.

Makes 4 servings.

Variation: For a rich whiting soup, follow the procedure
for rich soups. Shred the beef, cut the whiting, scallion,
garlic and bean cake. Heat 1 tablespoon sesame oil in a
pot and brown the meat, fish, scallion and garlic. Do
not brown the bean cake. Add the stock and daenchang.
Add the bean cake just before serving.

MALGUN MIOK KUK
CLEAR SEAWEED SOUP

After a baby is born the mother stays home for 21 days, and for this period of time, she must eat seaweed soup at least twice daily, and sometimes 3 or 4 times a day! Obviously, there cannot be too much of a good thing!

1 cup cut seaweed	4 cups water
½ pound beef (shoulder)	1 teaspoon soy sauce
1 scallion	1 tablespoon salt
1 clove garlic	

1. Soak the dried seaweed in warm water for 30 minutes, then rinse and wash carefully by hand. If necessary, cut out the hard line down the center. Cut the seaweed into 2-inch lengths. Shred the beef into 2-inch lengths. Cut the scallion into 2-inch lengths. Crush the garlic.

2. Bring the water to a boil. Add the beef and again bring to a boil. Remove the froth. Add the seaweed, scallion, garlic, soy sauce and salt. Lower the flame and simmer for 10 minutes.

Makes 4 servings.

Note: Gauge the amount of seaweed needed. Remember that dried foods always increase in volume once they have been soaked.

GINCHANG KUK
RICH SEAWEED SOUP

Seaweeds vary considerably in texture from one variety to another and the flavor is quite different as well. All seaweeds, whatever the taste, are highly nutritious. Koreans have valued them for centuries and seaweed soup is an item which finds its way to the table often.

1 cup cut seaweed	1 tablespoon sesame oil
½ pound beef (shoulder)	1 teaspoon soy sauce
1 scallion	1 tablespoon salt
1 clove garlic	4 cups water

1. Soak the dried seaweed in warm water for 30 minutes. Rinse and wash carefully by hand. If necessary, cut out the hard line down the center. Cut or break the seaweed into 2-inch lengths. Shred the beef into 2-inch lengths. Cut the scallion into 2-inch lengths and crush the garlic.

2. Heat the sesame oil in a heavy-bottomed pot. Brown the meat, then add the scallion, garlic, soy sauce and salt. Stir-fry for 30 seconds. Add the water, then the seaweed. Bring to a boil, reduce the heat and place a tight-fitting lid on the pot. Simmer for 10 minutes. Do not remove the lid from the pot until ready to serve.

Makes 4 servings.

KONG NAMUL KUK
YELLOW BEAN SPROUT SOUP

Large, yellow bean sprouts are needed for this soup. These sprouts have a larger body than the common variety and must be asked for specifically. The small sprouts make a *good* soup; the large sprouts have a distinctive flavor and make a *remarkable* soup. An old wives' tale has it that Kong Namul Kuk is good for those suffering from the flu. For some reason, possibly its low cost, it is a standby in Korea's army barracks.

¾ pound large bean sprouts	1 tablespoon sesame oil
½ pound flank steak	6 cups cold water
2 scallions	1 teaspoon soy sauce
2 cloves garlic	2 teaspoon salt
	dash black pepper

1. If small sprouts are used, wash them under cold water. If the large sprouts are used, clean as for string beans. Remove any black heads and the small root at the end of the stem.

2. Use the fatty end of the flank steak. (For certain soups a higher fat content is desirable.) Slice the steak thin, on the bias, using the full width of the steak. Slice again into very thin strips. Cut the scallions into 2-inch lengths, including the greens. Slice the garlic.

3. Place the sprouts, meat, scallion, garlic and sesame oil in a pot with a tight-fitting lid. Add the cold water. Bring to a boil and cook for 1 hour without removing the lid. Before serving add the soy sauce, salt and pepper.

Makes 2 to 5 servings.

MALGUN SIGUMCHI KUK
CLEAR SPINACH SOUP

½ pound fresh spinach   ½ pound ground beef
1 scallion   1 teaspoon soy sauce
1 clove garlic   1 tablespoon salt
4 cups water   dash pepper

1. Wash the spinach thoroughly and trim off the thick stems. Chop the scallion. Mince the garlic.

2. Bring the water to a boil. Add the meat and bring to a second boil. Skim off the froth. Add the spinach, scallion, garlic, soy sauce, salt and pepper. Lower the flame and simmer for 10 minutes. Serve immediately.

Makes 4 servings.

GINCHANG SIGUMCHI KUK
RICH SPINACH SOUP

½ pound fresh spinach   1 teaspoon soy sauce
1 scallion   1 tablespoon salt
1 clove garlic   dash pepper
1 tablespoon sesame oil   4 cups water
½ pound ground beef

1. Wash the spinach thoroughly, then trim off the thick
stems. Chop the scallion and mince the garlic.

2. Heat the sesame oil in a heavy-bottomed pot. Brown
the ground beef, separating the particles while stir-frying.
Add the scallion, garlic, soy sauce, salt and pepper
and stir-fry for 30 seconds. Add the water, then the
spinach. Bring the soup to a boil, then lower the flame.
Place a tight-fitting lid on the pot. Do not remove
the cover until soup is ready to be served.
Simmer for 10 minutes.

Makes 4 servings.

SIGUMCHI DAENCHANG KUK
SPINACH SOUP WITH BROWN SAUCE

¼ pound lean beef   ½ pound fresh spinach
  (shoulder, chuck or   ¼ cup daenchang
  flank)   4 cups beef stock

1. Shred the beef into 2-inch lengths. Wash the spinach thoroughly.

2. Mix the daenchang and stock in a cooking pot. Add the meat and bring the stock to a boil. Skim off the froth, add the spinach and continue cooking for 5 minutes.

Makes 4 servings.

Variation: For a rich spinach soup with brown sauce, follow the procedure for rich soups. Shred the beef, wash the spinach and heat 1 tablespoon sesame oil in a pot. Brown the meat and spinach briefly, then add the daenchang and the stock.

YANGPA DAENCHANG KUK
ONION SOUP WITH BROWN SAUCE

¼ pound lean beef   ¼ cup daenchang
  (shoulder)   4 cups beef stock
2 large onions

1. Shred the beef into 2-inch lengths. Cut the onions in half, then slice them into ¼-inch widths.

2. Mix the daenchang and the stock in a cooking pot. Add the meat and onion slices. Bring the mixture to a boil, skim off the froth and continue cooking for 5 minutes.

Makes 4 servings.

Variation: For a rich onion soup, follow the procedure for rich soups. Shred the beef, cut the onions and heat 1 tablespoon sesame oil in a pot. Brown the meat and onions, then add the stock and daenchang.

PA DAENCHANG KUK
SCALLION SOUP WITH BROWN SAUCE

¼ pound lean beef   ¼ cup daenchang
   (shoulder)   4 cups beef stock
6 scallions

1. Shred the beef into 2-inch lengths. Cut the scallions into 2-inch lengths.

2. Mix the daenchang and the stock in a cooking pot. Add the meat and scallions. Bring the mixture to a boil, skim off the froth and continue cooking for 5 minutes.

Makes 4 servings.

Variation: For a rich scallion soup, follow the procedure for rich soups. Shred the beef, cut the scallions and heat 1 tablespoon sesame oil in a pot. Brown the meat and scallions, then add the stock and daenchang.

BAECHU DAENCHANG KUK
CHINESE CABBAGE SOUP WITH BROWN SAUCE

¼ pound lean beef (shoulder, flank or round)

2 cups cut Chinese cabbage
¼ cup daenchang
4 cups beef stock

1. Shred the beef into 2-inch lengths. Wash the cabbage leaves and slice across them at 1-inch intervals.

2. Mix the daenchang and the stock in a cooking pot. Add the meat and bring the stock to a boil. Skim off the froth, then add the Chinese cabbage and continue cooking for 10 minutes.

Makes 4 servings.

Variations: For a rich Chinese cabbage soup, follow the procedure for rich soups. Shred the beef, cut the cabbage and heat 1 tablespoon sesame oil in a pot. Brown the meat and cabbage briefly, then add the stock and daenchang.

Use American cabbage cut into 1-inch squares.

MALGUN CHANG KUK
CLEAR TURNIP SOUP

½ pound lean beef
   (shoulder, shin or flank)
1 cup cut Chinese turnip
1 scallion

1 clove garlic
4 cups beef stock
1 teaspoon soy sauce
1 tablespoon salt

1. Shred the beef into 2-inch lengths. Peel the turnip, cut
it into 2-inch pieces, then slice. Cut the scallion into
2-inch lengths and mince the garlic.

2. Bring the stock to a boil. Add the beef and bring to a
boil a second time. Skim off the froth and add the turnip,
scallion, garlic, soy sauce and salt. Lower the flame
and simmer for 30 minutes.

Makes 4 servings.

Variation: For a rich turnip soup, follow the procedure for
rich soups. Heat 1 tablespoon sesame oil in a heavy-
bottomed pot and brown the meat. Add the turnip,
scallion and garlic. Add the soy sauce and salt, then the
stock. Bring the soup to a boil. Simmer for 20 minutes.

MU DAENCHANG KUK
TURNIP SOUP WITH BROWN SAUCE

¼ pound lean beef
   (shoulder, chuck or
   flank)

1 cup sliced Chinese
   turnip
¼ cup daenchang
4 cups beef stock

1. Shred the beef into 2-inch lengths. Slice the turnip thin into 2-inch lengths.

2. Mix the daenchang and the stock in a cooking pot. Add the meat and bring the stock to a boil. Skim off the froth, add the turnip slices and continue cooking for 30 minutes.

Makes 4 servings.

Variation: For a rich turnip soup follow the procedure for rich soups. Shred the beef, cut the turnip and heat 1 tablespoon sesame oil in a pot. Brown the meat and turnip briefly, then add the stock and daenchang.

MU CHUNGOL
TURNIP AND MIXED SOUP

This light but filling soup is quick and simple to prepare.
It may accompany a large dinner or serve as the main dish
for a family supper.

½ pound flank steak
½ pound Chinese turnip
4 fresh mushrooms
2 medium onions
4 scallions
2 cakes bean curd
1 cup or ½ pound
   transparent noodles

3 cups beef broth
2 teaspoons sesame oil
1 tablespoon salt
dash black pepper
2 eggs
10 pine nuts

1. Remove all the fat from a cut of flank steak or any
other tender cut of beef. Slice the meat paper-thin across
the grain on the bias. Slice again into thin strips across
the grain.

2. Slice the turnip into thin circles, then into thin
matchstick-shaped pieces. Slice the mushrooms, onions
and scallions in the same manner. The bean cakes should
be cut into thick finger-shaped pieces about ½ inch
wide. (Otherwise they will disintegrate during the
cooking.)

3. Cook the transparent noodles for 5 minutes, drain
and rinse under cold water. Cut them 2 or 3 times.

4. Place the meat, then the turnip, scallions, onions, noodles, bean cakes and mushrooms in the bottom of a pot. Add the broth to these ingredients and season with the sesame oil, salt and pepper. Bring to a boil and cook for 10 minutes.

5. Break the eggs on top of the soup, turn off the heat and cover the pot for a few minutes. The eggs should not be stirred. Decorate with pine nuts.

Makes 2 to 5 servings.

MU TANG
TURNIP SOUP WITH BEAN CURD

¼ pound lean beef
  (shoulder, chuck,
  round, flank or shin)
1 cup cut Chinese turnip
1 cake bean curd
1 scallion

1 clove garlic
1 tablespoon sesame oil
1 teaspoon soy sauce
1 tablespoon salt
4 cups beef stock

1. Slice the beef thin against the grain, then cut it into
1½-inch squares. Slice the turnip thin into 1-inch squares.
Chop the bean curd into ½-inch cubes. Cut the scallion
into 1-inch lengths. Mince the garlic.

2. Heat the sesame oil in a heavy-bottomed pot. Brown
the beef, then add the turnip, scallion and garlic. Add the
soy sauce, salt, then stock. Bring the soup to a boil.
Reduce the heat, cover the pot and let the soup simmer.
After 20 minutes of simmering, add the bean curd and
cook for only 2 minutes before serving.

Makes 4 servings.

DUBU DAENCHANG CHIGAE
BEAN CURD SOUP WITH BROWN SAUCE

¼ pound pork (shoulder
   or chops)
1 scallion
2 onions

2 cakes bean curd
2 cups water
2 tablespoons daenchang

1. Slice the pork thin against the grain, then cut it into
1-inch squares. Slice the scallion into 1½-inch lengths.
Slice the onions into ¼-inch widths and the bean curd
into ½-inch widths.

2. Arrange the pork slices on the bottom of a cooking
pot. Add the onions, scallion and bean curd. Mix the
daenchang with the water and pour over the ingredients.
Bring the mixture to a boil. Cook, covered, for 5 minutes.

Makes 2 to 4 servings.

Variation: If a hot soup is desired, substitute 2 to 3
tablespoons kochu chang (See page 263) for the
daenchang.

YACHAE CHIGAE
HOT VEGETABLE SOUP

Chigae, a thick, hot-tasting soup, requires generous
helpings of rice to balance its spicy taste.

¼ pound tender beef	5 mushrooms
½ pound red snapper	4 cups beef broth
1 cup Chinese cabbage	4 tablespoons kochu
1 cake bean curd	chang (See page 263)
3 scallions	2 eggs

1. Slice the beef into thin strips. Cut the red snapper into
1½-inch squares. Cut the cabbage into 1½-inch squares,
the bean cake into 1-inch squares and the scallions
into 2-inch lengths. Slice the mushrooms in half.

2. Arrange the cabbage on the bottom of the pot, then
add the cut ingredients. Pour the broth over all. Stir in the
kochu chang and boil vigorously for 15 minutes. Stir in 2
slightly beaten eggs just before serving.

Makes 2 to 6 servings.

Variations: The ingredients given are only suggestions. Left-over chicken, pork or beef bones which have a little meat on them can be boiled for 15 minutes to make a broth. Any vegetable may be added. It is always a good idea to use onions. Zucchini are particularly recommended as are potatoes, turnips and eggplant.

Use 2 cups beef broth for a thicker soup.

NOK DU KUK
GREEN BEAN SOUP

This recipe resembles a thick pea soup, although its color is a more vivid green. It is very bland, but has a delicate flavor.

½ pound or 1 cup round
   green beans in 2 cups
   water

7 cups water
1 cup beef stock
2 teaspoons salt

1. Soak the beans for 24 hours in 2 cups water.

2. Mix the beans and water in a blender until they have the consistency of a thick paste. Pour into a strainer placed over a large bowl. Put the beans remaining in the strainer back into the blender. Slowly add 2 cups water. Strain. Repeat this process until the 7 cups water have been used and the bean pulp is almost entirely absorbed. Discard the pulp that will not go through the strainer.

3. Bring the bean and water mixture to a boil. Stir frequently so that the mixture does not adhere to the bottom of the pan. Add the beef stock. Cook for 15 to 20 minutes. Season with salt to taste.

Makes 8 to 10 servings.

KAE KUK
SESAME SEED SOUP

Do not be deterred by the necessity of straining the
sesame seeds in this recipe. The result is well worth the
effort.

¾ pound sesame seeds   2 cups water
3 cups cold water   2 cups water
1 1-pound chicken   1½ teaspoons salt
3 cups water   dash black pepper
1 cup water

1. Soak the sesame seeds in 3 cups cold water for 24
hours.

2. Place the whole chicken in a pot. Cover with 3 cups
water. Bring to a boil, then skim off the froth carefully.
Simmer for 20 minutes.

3. Meanwhile drain the sesame seeds. Pour 1 cup water
into a blender, add the seeds and blend until very fine.
Place a strainer over a large bowl and strain complete
contents of blender, while shaking the strainer back and
forth. Return any seeds that have not gone through the
strainer to the blender. Add 2 cups water and blend until
very fine. Strain again. Repeat process one more time.
Now most of the seeds should have gone through the
strainer.

4. Add the sesame liquid to the chicken broth. (Do not remove the bones.) Bring to a boil. The mixture will resemble curdled milk. Stir for the first few minutes until the curdled-milk appearance disappears. Cover the pot and simmer for 1 hour.

5. Remove the bones and chicken. Add the salt and pepper. Taste. Add more salt, if necessary.

Makes 6 to 8 servings.

MEAT

BUL KOGI
BARBECUED BEEF

Bul Kogi is so popular that many Koreans consider it the national meat dish.

2 pounds sirloin steak	¼ cup sugar
3 scallions	2 tablespoons sherry
4 cloves garlic	¼ cup beef stock
5 tablespoons soy sauce	(optional)
2 tablespoons sesame oil	⅛ teaspoon black pepper

1. Slice the steak very thin on the bias. Score each piece with an X.

2. Chop the scallions and crush the garlic. Combine these ingredients with the remaining seasonings in a bowl. Add the meat to the marinade and mix well until all sides of the steak are coated.

3. The meat may be grilled immediately. The best results are obtained if the steak is marinated for 2 hours. The marinade will keep overnight.

Makes 4 servings.

Variation: Use rib steak or flank steak.

SOGOGI SANJUK
SKEWERED BEEF

Skewered beef is not a spicy dish; it has a very delicate
flavor. Metal skewers are available in most supermarkets,
but to capture the Korean mood, small wooden ones,
which may be purchased in Oriental food stores,
are recommended.

½ pound flank steak	1 tablespoon sesame oil
4 scallion stalks	1 tablespoon sherry
1 small carrot	1 teaspoon salt
1 clove garlic	dash black pepper
1 tablespoon sesame seeds	

1. Slice the steak across the grain into 3-inch lengths,
using the entire thickness of the steak. Cut off the green
ends of the scallions, retaining 3 inches of the white
part. Slice or quarter the carrot into 3-inch lengths.

2. Crush the garlic and combine all the seasonings in a
bowl. Add the steak and vegetables and mix well until
all sides of·the steak are coated.

3. Arrange the meat and vegetables on the skewers and grill. The carrots should still be crunchy when the meat is done.

Makes 4 small skewers.

Variation: Use sirloin steak or any tender cut.

KALBI KUI
MARINATED SHORT RIBS

4 extra large short ribs
2 large scallions, including
   green stems
2 large cloves garlic
½ cup soy sauce
¼ cup sesame oil
1 teaspoon sesame seeds

¼ teaspoon white
   vinegar
2 tablespoons sugar
¼ teaspoon dry hot
   mustard
¼ teaspoon black pepper

1. Trim the excess fat from the short ribs. Score the meat deeply every ½ inch, almost to the bone. Mince the scallions and garlic. Combine them with the remaining ingredients to make the marinade. Pour the marinade over the ribs, allowing it to penetrate to the bone. Turn the ribs over, so that the scored side is face-down in the sauce. Cover, allow to stand for 2 hours or refrigerate overnight, if possible.

2. Broil over charcoal or under an oven grill. If barbecued over charcoal, the ribs may be removed and the cooked outside pieces eaten, with the ribs then returned to the fire for additional cooking. If broiled in the oven, the ribs must be cooked longer. The outside becomes crisp and cooks more rapidly than the meat which is closer to the bone. Cooking time is about 15 minutes.

Makes 4 servings.

BANG JA KUI
ROAST BEEF

This recipe is not roast beef in the American sense, but is
a beef dish prepared with small slices of marinated
and grilled meat.

Bang Ja is the Korean word for "valet"—and this dish is
named for the servant who must catch a quick meal
while his master is enjoying himself at the dining room
table. Today although Korean valets are scarce, Bang Ja
is eaten by everyone.

½ pound rib meat (the piece on top of the fillet)
2 scallions
2 cloves garlic

2 tablespoons sesame oil
1 tablespoon beef stock
½ teaspoon salt
dash black pepper

1. Cut the meat into 3 or 4 slices about ½ inch thick.
Score the beef on both sides in a diamond shape. Mince
the scallions and crush the garlic.

2. Combine the remaining ingredients in a bowl. Add the
garlic, scallions and beef slices. Mix well until all sides
of the meat are coated.

3. Grill.

Makes 2 servings.

NUBI ANI
GRILLED STEAK

Grilled steak is slightly sweet-tasting and should be served rare.

½ pound sirloin steak
2 scallions
2 cloves garlic
2 tablespoons sesame oil

1 tablespoon sesame
  seeds
2 tablespoons sugar
½ teaspoon salt
dash black pepper

1. Cut the meat into 2 pieces about 1 inch thick, then score each diagonally at ½-inch intervals. Score on the other side on the opposite diagonal. Mince the scallions and garlic.

2. Combine all the seasonings in a bowl. Add the steak slices and mix well until all sides of the steak are coated.

3. Marinate or grill immediately over a charcoal or an electric grill. An oven broiler may be used.

Makes 2 servings.

KALBI KUI
SHORT RIBS IN SWEET SAUCE

Ideally, all short ribs should be broiled over charcoal. Grilling chars the outside of the ribs, while the inside remains tender and pink.

1½ pounds short ribs ¼ cup soy sauce
2 scallions 2 tablespoons sugar
1 tablespoon sesame oil dash black pepper
1 teaspoon sesame seeds

1. Have the ribs cut into 3-inch lengths. Trim off the excess fat. If the ribs are thin, cross-score to the bone, as for a ham. If the ribs are over 1½ inches thick, slice as thin as possible, across the grain down to the bone.

2. Mince the scallions and combine with the remaining ingredients in a bowl or in a small roasting pan. Add the ribs and mix well, coating all sides of the ribs with the marinade.

3. Grill immediately or cover and let marinate until ready to serve. The cooking time will vary depending on how well the meat is cooked and the heat of the grill. A charcoal grill is suggested, but an electric grill or an oven broiler may be used.

Makes 2 to 4 servings.

SOGOM KALBI KUI
SHORT RIBS IN SALT SAUCE

Short ribs are ideal for outdoor barbecuing and for casual picnics. The preparation can be done in advance. An electric grill may be used.

1½ pounds short ribs	1 tablespoon sesame
2 scallions	seeds
2 to 3 cloves garlic	1 teaspoon salt
	dash black pepper

1. Have the ribs cut into 3-inch lengths. Trim off the excess fat. If the ribs are thin, cross-score to the bone, as for a ham. If the ribs are over 1½ inches thick, slice as thin as possible, across the grain down to the bone.

2. Mince the scallions and crush the garlic. Combine them with the remaining ingredients in a bowl. Add the ribs and mix well until all sides of the ribs are coated.

3. Grill immediately or cover and let marinate until ready to serve. The cooking time depends on the heat of the grill and how well the meat is cooked.

Makes 2 to 4 servings.

YUK SANJUK CHUNYUA
KOREAN HAMBURGER

Korean hamburger is a tasty appetizer or a side dish. It is
usually made with equal amounts of beef and pork;
beef is the tastier, and pork is the more tender of the two
—the combination of both is just right. Bean curd or
bread crumbs keep the hamburger soft and moist.

¼ pound ground beef	1 teaspoon sesame seeds
¼ pound ground pork	2 teaspoons sesame oil
⅛ pound bean curd or 2 inches of bean curd cake or bread crumbs	½ teaspoon salt dash pepper
2 cloves garlic, crushed	3 tablespoons flour
1 scallion, minced	2 eggs, slightly beaten
	⅓ cup sesame oil

1. Mix the ground meat and all the seasonings well in a
bowl. Roll the meat into 12 small flat hamburger patties
and dredge them in the flour. Using the thumb and
forefinger, make a small depression in the center of each
one. This hollow will prevent shrinkage while cooking.

2. Heat the oil in a skillet to 400 degrees. Dip the
hamburger patties into the eggs, then sauté them in the
hot oil until browned.

Makes 12 small hamburger patties or 4 servings as
an appetizer.

Variations: Use ½ pound ground beef or ½ pound ground pork or ½ pound ground chicken (a young chicken is preferred).

YUK SANJUK KUI
GRILLED HAMBURGER

Although grilled hamburger is similar in seasoning to
Korean hamburger, the methods of preparation produce
distinctly different tastes.

¼ pound ground beef
¼ pound ground pork
2 cloves garlic
1 scallion
⅛ pound bean curd
   (about 2 inches)

1 teaspoon sesame seeds
2 teaspoons sesame oil
½ teaspoon salt
1 tablespoon sugar
dash pepper

1. Crush the garlic and mince the scallion. Combine with
the ground meat and the rest of the ingredients in a bowl.
Mix well. Roll the meat into 6 flat hamburger patties.

2. Grill the meat over a charcoal or an electric grill. If
neither of these is available, use a broiler.

Makes 2 to 4 servings.

Variations: Use ½ pound ground beef or ½ pound
ground pork or ½ pound ground chicken.

Substitute bread crumbs for the bean curd.

SOGOGI ALSSAM
BEEF OMELET

Because it is relatively dry, this omelet is often to be
found in students' lunch boxes or on picnics.

¼ pound beef (chuck)	1 tablespoon sesame oil
1 scallion	¼ teaspoon salt
1 clove garlic	dash black pepper
8 eggs	1 teaspoon sesame oil

1. Mince the beef fine. Mince the scallion and garlic.
Break the eggs in a separate bowl and beat them slightly.

2. Heat the tablespoon sesame oil in a heavy skillet.
While browning the meat, add the scallion, garlic, salt
and pepper. Then add the browned meat to the eggs.

3. Heat the teaspoon sesame oil in a skillet. Add the eggs
and meat mixture and make an omelet. Instead of turning
the omelet over, cook the top by placing the skillet
under a broiler for a few moments. Remove to a serving
platter and cool slightly. Then roll the omelet tightly.
Slice into circles 2 inches wide.

Makes 4 servings.

Variations: Substitute ¼ pound ground or minced pork
for the beef.

Substitute ¼ pound ground or minced chicken or
the equivalent of one chicken breast for the beef.

Substitute ¼ pound ground chuck for the beef.

Substitute one small bunch of Chinese chives for the beef and scallion and garlic seasonings. The recipe then becomes an *omelet aux fines herbes.*

SOKKORI CHIM
OXTAIL STEW

Oxtail is one of the tastiest cuts of meat; served as a stew it is absolutely delicious. This recipe may be prepared the day or morning before the dinner and reheated at the last minute. Although oxtail stew is flavorful, it is not spicy. The sauce should have the consistency of a thin gravy.

4 oxtails	6 scallions
8 cups cold water	1 tablespoon sesame
6 slices, 2 inches thick of	seeds
Chinese turnip	1 tablespoon sesame oil
(optional)	dash black pepper
6 cloves garlic	1 tablespoon salt
6 mushrooms	1 tablespoon soy sauce

1. Cover the oxtails with 8 cups cold water and a tight-fitting lid. Bring to a boil, skim off the froth and cook for 2½ hours or until the meat can be removed from the bone with a fork. The broth should have boiled down to about 2 cups. If there is too much liquid left, remove the lid from the pot and boil the liquid down. If the turnip is used, the slices should be dropped into boiling water for a moment, strained, then added to the oxtail. Allow the broth to cool so that the fat can be removed. Also remove any excess fat from the larger pieces of oxtail.

2. Slice the garlic and the mushrooms. Cut the scallions into 2-inch lengths and add these ingredients to the meat along with the sesame seeds, sesame oil, ajinomoto and pepper. The salt should be added to the broth in small quantities and tasted. Add the soy sauce for color.

3. Reheat the seasoned oxtails in the broth and serve steaming.

Makes 4 servings.

Variation: As a side dish, use 1 oxtail, 8 cups cold water, 3 slices Chinese turnip, 2 cloves garlic, 2 mushrooms, 2 scallions, 1 teaspoon sesame oil, dash black pepper, 1 teaspoon salt and 1 tablespoon soy sauce.

Makes 1-4 servings.

UHBUK JAENGBAN
BOILED BEEF

Boiled beef is simple to prepare; the meat may be boiled the night before. Before serving, the beef may be sliced, the sauce added and the whole recipe warmed in a chafing dish. Perfect for a buffet, boiled beef is mild-tasting and should appeal to everyone.

Basic

2 pounds flank steak	10 cups water

Sauce

¼ scallion	1 teaspoon sesame oil
2 cloves garlic	1 tablespoon soy sauce
1 cup beef broth	½ teaspoon salt
1 teaspoon sesame seeds	dash black pepper

Decoration

2 egg whites	¼ teaspoon salt
2 egg yolks	small amount oil

Basic
If possible, leave the flank steak whole. Place the meat in a pot and cover with 10 cups cold water and a tight-fitting lid. Bring to a boil, skim off the froth and boil rapidly for about 2 hours or until the meat is tender. There should be only 1 cup of liquid remaining. If there is more than this amount left, remove the meat and boil

down the liquid with the lid off. Reserve the remaining liquid for the sauce. Cool the meat for at least 1 hour or overnight, if convenient. Trim off any fat, then slice thin on a diagonal. Arrange on a platter or in a chafing dish.

Sauce
Chop the scallion and crush the garlic. Add the seasonings for the sauce to 1 cup broth from the flank steak and simmer for 5 minutes. Pour the broth over the meat.

Decoration
1. Separate the yolks from the whites of 2 eggs. Beat the yolks slightly and add ⅛ teaspoon salt to both the whites and the yolks

2. Grease a heavy skillet lightly with oil. Make a thin pancake with the yolks, then another with the whites. Slice both pancakes into thin threads, being careful to keep them separate.

3. Arrange the decorations on top of the meat in little piles, or put a pile of whites in the center, surrounding it by 3 piles of yolks. If the chafing dish is not used, the decoration must be ready before the meat is sliced or the sauce is added. This dish should be served hot.

Makes 4 servings.

KALBI CHIM
SHORT RIBS STEW

2½ pounds short ribs   1 teaspoon sesame oil
6 cups cold water   1 tablespoon sugar
2 cloves garlic   dash black pepper
2 mushrooms   salt to taste
2 scallions   1 tablespoon soy sauce
1 teaspoon sesame seeds

1. Cover the short ribs with 6 cups cold water. Bring to a boil, skim off the froth and cook for 2 hours or until the meat is very tender. The broth should have boiled down to 2 cups.

2. Slice the garlic and mushroms. Cut the scallions into 2-inch lengths and add these ingredients to the stew along with the sesame seeds, sesame oil, sugar and pepper. Salt the broth sparingly and taste. Add the soy sauce.

3. Reheat the seasoned stew and serve steaming.

Makes 2 to 4 servings.

SOGOGI PYUNYUK
BOILED BEEF IN SAUCE

Boiled beef is easy to prepare and may be served in a chafing dish. Its delicious flavor is mild, yet distinctive.

2 pounds boneless beef shin	1 cup beef stock
1 tablespoon onion	1 teaspoon cornstarch
1 scallion	1 tablespoon soy sauce
1 clove garlic	1 carrot

1. Boil the beef for 2 hours. (See the directions for oxtail and beef soup stock.) Allow it to cool, then slice the beef into pieces ¼ inch thick.

2. Mince the onion and scallion. Slice the garlic. Combine these 3 seasonings with the remaining ingredients in a pan and boil for 3 minutes.

3. Pour the sauce over the meat and decorate with a carrot cut on the bias into thin slices.

Makes 4 servings.

Variations: One oxtail may be added to the beef shin.

A delicate tasting soup can be prepared by adding salt, a tablespoon of soy sauce and some minced scallions to the broth.

WANJA BOKUM
MEATBALLS IN SAUCE

Simple and economical to prepare, these meatballs may
be cooked in advance and reheated in their sauce,
perhaps in a chafing dish. If many guests are expected, the
recipe may easily be doubled or quadrupled.

Meatballs

1 pound ground beef
    (good quality chuck or
    round)
3 cloves garlic
½ teaspoon salt

1 teaspoon sesame seeds
1 teaspoon sesame oil
1 tablespoon flour
2 tablespoons salad oil

Sauce

2 cloves garlic
5 small fresh mushrooms
½ carrot
1 small onion
½ scallion
1 tablespoon sesame oil

¾ cup beef stock
1 tablespoon soy sauce
dash black pepper
½ tablespoon cornstarch
½ cup beef stock

Decoration

egg decoration (See
    page 266)

10 pine nuts

Sauce
1. Slice the garlic and the mushrooms, including the stems. Slice the carrot thin on a diagonal. Quarter the onion, then peel off the layers one by one. Cut the scallion into 4 pieces on a diagonal.

2. Heat the sesame oil in a saucepan. Brown the garlic, onion and scallion lightly. Add the beef stock, soy sauce, mushrooms and carrot. Season with the pepper and allow to simmer slowly.

3. Combine the cornstarch with the remaining stock in a bowl. Slowly blend this mixture into the sauce until it reaches the desired consistency.

Make the egg decoration.

Meatballs
1. Crush the garlic and mix with the ground beef, salt, sesame seeds and sesame oil. Shape the beef into meatballs the size of a walnut. Coat the meatballs lightly, rolling them in the flour.

2. Heat the salad oil in a heavy skillet until very hot. Add the meatballs and shake them vigorously in the pan, coating all sides with the oil. Do not let meatballs stick to the pan. Cook them until well browned.

3. Add the meatballs to the sauce and reheat to mix the juices. Garnish with the egg decoration and pine nuts.

Makes 2 to 4 servings.

Variations: The meatballs may be made with ground pork or a mixture of ground beef and pork. The flavor may be varied by using ground chicken. Part or all of a beaten egg may be needed to keep the chicken together. If chicken is used, substitute chicken stock for beef stock.

DDUK BOKUM
RICE CAKE AND BEEF SAUTEED

Rice cakes resemble compressed rice. Moist inside, their outer surfaces are smooth and firm to the touch. The cakes may be purchased in many Oriental grocery stores which stock fresh produce. Bland in appearance and taste and cooked in soy sauce, this recipe is similar to a Chinese dish.

½ cup soaked cloud-ear mushrooms
1 pound rice cake
¼ pound flank steak
2 cloves garlic
4 small fresh mushrooms
2 scallions
5 spinach leaves

¼ green pepper
1 tablespoon sesame oil
2 tablespoons soy sauce
2 tablespoons sugar
dash black pepper
1 cup beef broth
1 teaspoon potato starch
2 tablespoons water

1. Soak a dozen or more cloud-ear mushrooms in 1 cup warm water or use ½ cup packed soaked mushrooms.

2. Slice the rice cake into ½-inch thicknesses. Slice the flank steak very thin into pieces about 1-inch square. Shred the garlic into fine finger-shaped pieces. Slice the fresh mushrooms, but leave their stems attached. Cut the scallions into 1½-inch lengths. Wash the spinach leaves and remove the tough stems. Slice the green pepper on a diagonal into 4 pieces.

3. Heat the sesame oil in a frying pan. Brown the meat quickly by stir-frying, add the scallions, garlic and green pepper. Add the soy sauce, sugar and black pepper. Shake the pan a few times vigorously to combine the flavors and add the beef broth. While the liquid is bubbling, add the rice cake, both kinds of mushrooms and the spinach leaves. Cook for 5 minutes.

4. Dilute the potato starch in some cold water, then stir all the ingredients into the sauce to thicken slightly. Serve piping hot.

Makes 2 to 4 servings.

Variation: Substitute ¼ pound chicken or pork for the flank steak.

SOGOGI TWIKIM
DEEP FRIED BEEF STRIPS

½ pound flank steak
1 egg
¼ cup water
6 tablespoons cornstarch

½ teaspoon salt
3 cloves garlic
2 scallions
3 cups oil for frying

1. Slice the flank steak into pieces 2 inches long and
1 inch wide.

2. Beat together the egg and water in a bowl. Add the
cornstarch, salt and ajinomoto. Beat with chopsticks or a
fork until the mixture is smooth.

3. Crush or mince the garlic. Mince the scallions. Add
both ingredients to the cornstarch mixture. Add the beef
and mix well until all sides of the beef are coated.

4. Heat the oil to about 400 degrees. Drop the beef strips
one by one into the hot oil. Fry the beef strips for 1
minute and then remove them with a slotted spoon or
strainer. Return the beef to the cornstarch mixture and
coat all sides. Fry a second time in the hot oil until brown.
When the meat strips float to the top, they are done.
Strain the beef strips in the strainer or on paper towels.
Makes 2 to 4 servings.

SOGOGI CHANG CHORIM
BEEF MARINATED IN SOY SAUCE

This beef recipe may be served cold as a side dish.

1½ pounds beef shin	1 cup soy sauce
2 scallions	⅓ teaspoon cayenne
3 cloves garlic	pepper
1 cup beef stock	dash black pepper

1. Place the meat in a pot and cover with cold water. Bring to a boil and skim off the froth. Cover and simmer for 2 hours. Reserve the liquid for soup stock and cool the meat. Slice the beef into pieces about 1½ inches long and 1 inch wide.

2. Coarsely chop the scallions and garlic. Place the sliced meat into a pan with the scallions, garlic, beef stock and soy sauce. Bring to a boil. Season with the red and black pepper. Simmer for 5 minutes.

3. Refrigerate the beef in the sauce. The fat will rise to the top and can then be removed. The meat will keep indefinitely.

Makes 4 to 6 servings.

YUK WHE
RAW MEAT

Anyone who enjoys a steak tartare will probably like Yuk
Whe. Successful results are certain if the meat is sliced
into very thin pieces. Raw meat is traditionally served
with pears, which aid digestion.

1 pound sirloin steak	1 teaspoon soy sauce
2 cloves garlic	1 teaspoon sugar
1 tablespoon beef stock	1 teaspoon salt
1 tablespoon sesame oil	½ pear
1 teaspoon sesame seeds	10 pine nuts

1. Remove any fat from the meat. Slice the steak paper-
thin across the grain into pieces about 2½-inches square.
Cut each square again, also across the grain very fine
to make long strips.

2. Crush the garlic and add it to the meat along with the
stock, sesame oil, sesame seeds, soy sauce, sugar and
salt. *Just* before serving, peel a pear. Slice it thin into
finger-shaped pieces in the same manner as for the meat.
Arrange the meat on a platter, garnish with the
pear and sprinkle with coarsely chopped pine nuts.
Serve immediately.

Makes 4 servings.

CHAEYUK KUI
PORK ROAST

This dish is fairly spicy: it gets its highly seasoned flavor from kochee chang. Although the amount indicated below is recommended, it is possible to use a little less.

½ pound pork shoulder or other lean pork
2 scallions
1 clove garlic
1 tablespoon sesame oil

1 tablespoon sesame seeds
1 tablespoon sugar
dash black pepper
4 teaspoons kochu chang (See page 263)

1. Cut the pork into 4 or 5 slices about ¼ inch thick.

2. Mince the scallions. Mince or crush the garlic. Combine both ingredients with the remaining seasonings in a bowl. Add the pork slices and mix well until all sides of the pork are coated.

3. Grill immediately or marinate until ready to serve. It is important that the pork be well done; the outside should be dark, almost charred. A charcoal, an electric or an oven grill may be used.

Makes 2 to 4 servings.

CHAEYUK SANJUK
SKEWERED PORK

These skewers are simple to prepare. In the northern part of Korea, kimchi is often added to the skewers.

½ pound lean pork
4 scallions
1 small carrot
1 clove garlic
1 tablespoon sesame seeds

1 tablespoon sesame oil
1 tablespoon sherry
1 teaspoon salt
dash black pepper

1. Slice the pork into 3-inch lengths with a width of ½ to ¼ inches. Cut the scallions into 3-inch lengths, discarding the green ends. Slice or quarter the carrot into 3-inch lengths.

2. Crush the garlic and combine with the remaining ingredients in a bowl. Add the pork, carrot and scallion slices and mix well until all sides of the pork are covered.

3. Arrange on the skewers and grill. The pork, of course, should be well done.

Makes 4 small skewers.

CHAEKALBI PYUNCHUL KUI
PORK CHOPS IN SWEET SAUCE

These pork chops can be made in 15 minutes, yet they look as if they took hours of preparation. They are served whole along with a dark rich sauce.

Chops

4 pork chops (1½ to 2 pounds)

1 tablespoon sesame oil

Sauce

⅓ cup sherry
⅔ cup soy sauce
⅓ cup sugar
5 cloves garlic

2 pieces fresh ginger the size of walnuts (¼ cup when slivered)

1. Combine the sherry, soy sauce and sugar in a small saucepan. Cut the garlic cloves and ginger into thin slivers and add them to the sauce mixture. Bring these ingredients to a boil, then simmer for 10 minutes over a low flame.

2. Add enough sesame oil to cover the bottom of a heavy skillet. Heat the oil until very hot, then add the pork chops. Brown them on one side, being careful that they do not stick to the bottom of the pan. Turn the chops over and place a tight-fitting cover over them. When the pork is well browned on both sides and the meat is white, yet tender (pork is done when the meat loses all trace

of pink), add the sauce mixture and cook vigorously for 3 minutes. Keep turning the chops over in the sauce so that both sides are coated with the color and permeated with the flavor of the sauce.

3. Arrange the chops on a platter and pour the sauce over them. Serve immediately.

Makes 4 servings.

Variations: Decorate with hot red pepper, red bell or green bell peppers.

If this recipe is used as a main dish, double the amount of pork per person and use:

½ cup sherry	7 cloves garlic
1 cup soy sauce	⅓ cup ginger
½ cup sugar	

CHAEKALBI CHIM
SPARERIBS MARINATED IN SWEET SAUCE

1½ pounds spareribs of
   pork
2 scallions
1 teaspoon sesame seeds

1 tablespoon sesame oil
2 tablespoons sugar
¼ cup soy sauce
dash black pepper

1. Have the ribs cut in half crosswise. Cut each rib apart between each bone. Remove the excess fat. Slash the skin on the bones with the point of a knife. Score the meat deeply.

2. Mince the scallions and combine them with the remaining ingredients in a bowl or in a small rectangular pan, if marinating. Add the ribs and mix well until all sides of the ribs are coated with the marinade.

3. Grill the ribs immediately or cover and let marinate until ready to serve. An electric or a charcoal grill is the best cooking medium; however, an oven broiler may be used. The ribs should be crisp and well done. Cooking time will depend on the method used.

Makes 2 to 4 servings.

CHAEKALBI KOCHU CHANG KUI
SPARERIBS OF PORK IN RED SAUCE

The kochee chang used in this recipe imparts a spicy flavor and a distinctive aroma to the pork.

1 pound spareribs of pork
2 scallions
3 cloves garlic
4 teaspoons kochu chang
  (See page 263)
1 tablespoon sesame oil

1 tablespoon sesame
  seeds
1 tablespoon soy sauce
1 tablespoon sugar
dash black pepper

1. Separate the ribs and score the meat on either side. Make a slash down the center of the bone with the point of a knife. Score on both sides those parts which have no bone.

2. Mince the scallions and crush the garlic. Combine these ingredients with the remaining seasonings in a bowl. Add the ribs and mix well until all sides of the ribs are coated with the marinade.

3. Grill. The ribs should, of course, be well done. The outer edges may become slightly charred.

Makes 1 to 4 servings.

CHAEYUK TWIKIM
DEEP FRIED PORK STRIPS

½ pound lean pork
   shoulder
¼ cup water
1 egg
6 tablespoons cornstarch

½ teaspoon salt
3 cloves garlic
2 scallions
3 cups oil for frying

1. Slice the pork into pieces 2 inches long and 1 inch wide.

2. Beat the water and egg together in a bowl. Add the cornstarch and salt. Beat this mixture with chopsticks or a fork until smooth.

3. Crush or mince the garlic. Mince the scallions. Add the garlic and scallions to the cornstarch mixture. Then add the pork and mix well until all sides of the pork are coated.

4. Heat the oil in a skillet to about 400 degrees, then drop in the pork pieces one by one. (If they are all added at the same time, the temperature of the oil will be reduced drastically.) Fry the pork for 1 minute and then remove with a slotted spoon or strainer. Return the pork to the cornstarch mixture and coat all sides. Fry the pork a second time in the hot oil until brown. When the meat floats to the top, it is done. Strain in a strainer or on paper towels.

Makes 2 to 4 servings.

MU CHANGWUA
TURNIP AND PORK STEW

The flavor of turnip and pork stew is fairly strong.

½ pound pork	1 tablespoon cooking oil
½ pound Chinese turnip	¼ cup soy sauce
2 cloves garlic	¼ cup sherry
4 slices fresh ginger or 1	¾ cup beef stock
teaspoon powdered	1 teaspoon sugar

1. Cut the pork into slices 1½ inches long by 1 inch wide by ½ inch thick. Cut rounds of turnip ½ inch thick. Slice the garlic. If fresh ginger is used, slice the same amount of ginger as garlic (the equivalent of 2 cloves).

2. Parboil the turnip for 15 minutes. Strain and discard the water. Return the turnip to the pot.

3. Heat the oil in a skillet and brown the pork well over a high flame. Add the pork, garlic and ginger to the turnip. Pour the soy sauce and sherry over the ingredients and bring to a boil. Add the stock and sugar and cook for 20 to 30 minutes or until all moisture has been absorbed.

Makes 1 to 3 servings.

DAK BOKUM
STEWED CHICKEN

Stewed chicken is very mild-tasting and easy to prepare. It may be served as a main dish along with rice.

1 2 to 2½-pound chicken
2 small carrots
2 scallions
3 button mushrooms
3 cloves garlic
2 tablespoons sesame oil

1½ cups water
1 teaspoon salt
1 tablespoon soy sauce
1 onion
1 teaspoon cornstarch
¼ cup water

1. Cut the chicken into 2-inch squares. (Disjoint the wings, halve the breasts and legs.) Slice the carrots and the scallions into 2-inch lengths. Halve the mushrooms and slice the garlic.

2. Heat the oil in a heavy skillet. Brown the garlic slightly. Add the scallions and fry for a moment. Then add the chicken pieces. The liver and gizzard may be included; but if used, the gizzard should be scored first. Brown the chicken for 5 minutes over a high flame. Place a lid over the pan and continue browning for 5 minutes longer. Add the 1½ cups water, salt, soy sauce, carrots, onion and mushrooms. Simmer, covered, for 30 minutes, stirring from time to time.

3. Combine the cornstarch and the ¼ cup water in a bowl. This mixture should be thick enough to coat the chicken.

Makes 2 to 4 servings.

DAK CHORIM
CHICKEN IN SOY SAUCE

1 frying chicken, cut up
cornstarch for dredging
1 clove garlic
3 scallions

3 tablespoons sesame oil
¼ cup soy sauce
¼ cup chicken stock or
   water

1. Dredge the chicken parts in the cornstarch. Mince the garlic and halve the scallions.

2. Heat the oil in a heavy frying pan and brown the chicken parts until they are crisp. Add the soy sauce, stock, scallions and garlic. Cover and simmer slowly for about 20 minutes or until done. If necessary, add more water or stock to prevent the chicken from sticking to the pan.

Makes 4 servings.

DAK SANJUK
SKEWERED CHICKEN

½ pound of chicken
  breasts
4 scallions
1 small carrot
1 clove garlic

1 tablespoon sesame
  seeds
1 tablespoon sesame oil
1 tablespoon sherry
1 teaspoon salt
dash black pepper

1. Bone the chicken breasts and slice across the grain into 3-inch lengths. Cut the scallions into 3-inch lengths, discarding the green ends. Slice or quarter the carrot into 3-inch lengths.

2. Crush the garlic and combine with the remaining ingredients in a bowl. Add the chicken, carrot and scallions and mix well until all sides of the chicken are coated.

3. Arrange on skewers and grill.

Makes 4 small skewers.

DAK JINCHANG KUI
GRILLED CHICKEN WITH SOY SAUCE

Grilled chicken with soy sauce is a savory main dish,
prepared western style. It can be made quickly.

1 pound of chicken breasts	2 tablespoons sesame oil
2 scallions	2 teaspoons sesame seeds
2 cloves garlic	1 teaspoon sugar
2 tablespoons soy sauce	dash black pepper

1. Score the chicken breasts lightly against the grain. To
flatten, pound the breasts with the flat side of a knife.

2. Mince the scallions and mince or crush the garlic.
Combine these ingredients with the remaining seasonings
in a bowl and mix thoroughly. Add the chicken and mix
well until all sides of the breasts are coated.

3. Grill. As a main dish, serve the breasts whole; as a
side dish cut them into 2-inch lengths.

Makes 2 to 4 servings.

DAK KOCHU CHANG KUI
GRILLED CHICKEN IN RED SAUCE

1 pound chicken breasts
2 scallions
2 cloves garlic
2 tablespoons sherry
2 tablespoons sesame oil

2 teaspoons sesame seeds
2 tablespoons kochu
   chang (See page 263)
dash black pepper

1. Open the chicken breasts by scoring them lightly. To flatten, pound the breasts with the flat side of a knife.

2. Mince the scallions and mince or crush the garlic. Combine these ingredients with the remaining seasonings in a bowl. Add the chicken and mix well until all sides of the breasts are coated.

3. Grill. An open electric grill may be used, or the breasts may be barbecued.

Makes 2 to 4 servings.

DAK KUI
CHICKEN BREASTS IN RED SAUCE

This recipe is a spicy way of making chicken.

2 chicken breasts	1 tablespoon sesame
2 scallions	seeds
3 cloves garlic	1 tablespoon sugar
4 teaspoons kochu chang	1 tablespoon soy sauce
(See page 263)	dash black pepper
1 tablespoon sesame oil	

1. To flatten the chicken breasts, pound them with the flat side of a knife. Score them on a diagonal across the grain.

2. Mince the scallions and crush the garlic. Combine these ingredients with the remaining seasonings in a bowl. Add the chicken breasts and mix well until all sides of the breasts are coated with the marinade.

3. Grill. Be careful not to overcook the chicken, or it will become tough and stringy. Cut the breasts into 2-inch pieces and serve.

Makes 2 to 4 servings.

DAK TWIKIM
DEEP FRIED CHICKEN STRIPS

½ pound chicken breasts	½ teaspoon salt
1 egg	3 cloves garlic
¼ cup water	2 scallions
6 tablespoons cornstarch	3 cups oil for frying

1. Bone the chicken breasts and slice them across the grain into strips about 2 inches long and 1 inch wide.

2. Beat together the egg and water in a bowl. Add the cornstarch and salt. Beat with chopsticks or a fork until the mixture is smooth.

3. Crush or mince the garlic. Mince the scallions. Add these ingredients to the cornstarch mixture. Add the chicken and mix well until all sides of the chicken are coated.

4. Heat the oil to about 400 degrees. Drop the chicken strips one by one into the hot oil. Fry the strips for one minute and then remove them with a slotted spoon or strainer. Return the strips to the cornstarch mixture and coat all sides. Fry a second time in the hot oil until brown. When the chicken floats to the top, it is done. Strain the chicken strips in a strainer or on paper towels.

Makes 2 to 4 servings.

YUMTONG KUI
VEAL KIDNEY

Kidneys may be eaten raw. The longer they cook, the tougher they get and the less delicate they taste.

½ pound kidneys
1 scallion
1 to 2 cloves garlic
1 teaspoon sesame seeds

2 teaspoons sesame oil
2 tablespoons sherry
½ teaspoon salt

1. Slice the kidneys thin across the grain. Mince the scallion and crush the garlic. Combine these ingredients with the remaining seasonings in a bowl. Add the kidney slices and mix well until all sides of the kidneys are coated.
2. Grill. Remember to cook the kidneys briefly. They should not be too well done.

Makes 1 to 2 servings.

GAN CHUNYUA
LIVER SAUTEED IN EGG BATTER

½ pound liver, preferably
   calves' liver
½ teaspoon salt
dash pepper

3 tablespoons flour
1 egg
⅓ cup sesame oil

1. Slice the liver into thin bite-sized pieces. Score lightly and sprinkle with salt and pepper. Dredge the pieces in the flour, then dip them into a slightly beaten egg.

2. Heat the oil in a skillet until very hot. Sauté the liver for 1 minute on each side. Turn off the heat and let the liver stand for a few moments in the hot pan.

Makes 2 servings.

FISH

SAIWU BUCHIM
SAUTÉED SHRIMP

12 jumbo shrimp	2 tablespoons sesame oil
salt	2 eggs
pepper	¼ cup soy sauce
2 teaspoons sesame seeds	2 tablespoons vinegar
flour for dredging	

1. Shell and de-vein the shrimp. Slit the shrimp length-wise down the back without cutting all the way through the flesh. Leave the tail intact. Flatten the shrimp and sprinkle with salt, pepper and sesame seeds.
Dredge the shrimp in flour.

2. Heat the oil in a heavy frying pan. Beat the two eggs in a bowl. Dip the shrimp into the eggs and sauté for about 4 minutes or until golden on both sides. Serve with a side dish of soy sauce and vinegar for dipping.

Makes 4 servings.

Variation: Substitute prawns for shrimp.

SAIWU TONG KUI
GRILLED SHRIMP

By grilling the shrimp quickly in their shells, the shrimp taste remains intact. Unfortunately, so does the shell— happy picking!

6 jumbo shrimp	¼ teaspoon sesame seeds
1 tablespoon white wine	½ egg yolk
2 cloves garlic	¾ teaspoon salt
1 teaspoon sesame oil	

1. Score each shrimp lightly between each set of legs. There should be 3 scores on the stomach side. Split each shrimp gingerly down the center of the back, being careful not to cut it in two. Flatten the shrimp and remove any waste matter.

2. Crush the garlic, then mix it well with the wine, sesame oil, sesame seeds, egg yolk and salt in a bowl.
(The white wine will make the fish shine when broiled.)

3. Dip the shrimp into the mixture until both sides are well coated. Grill the shrimp with the shell side turned down toward the heat first. This sequence will prevent the shrimp from curling up.

Makes 2 servings.

SAIWU ALSSAM
SHRIMP OMELET

4 jumbo shrimp	¼ teaspoon salt
1 scallion	dash black pepper
1 clove garlic	8 eggs
1 tablespoon sesame oil	1 teaspoon sesame oil

1. Shell, de-vein and wash the shrimp, then mince them fine. Mince the scallion and the garlic. Break the eggs in a separate bowl and beat them slightly.

2. Heat the sesame oil in a heavy skillet. Brown the shrimp, adding the garlic, scallion, salt and pepper. Then add the brown shrimp mixture to the eggs.

3. Heat the remaining sesame oil in a skillet. Add the eggs and shrimp mixture and make an omelet in the usual manner. Instead of turning the mixture over, cook the top by placing the skillet under the broiler for a few moments. Remove to a serving platter and cool slightly. Roll the omelet tightly. Slice into circles 2 inches wide.

Makes 4 servings.

DAEHAP CHIM
SHINING SHELLFISH WITH PORK

Shellfish and pork are combined in a delightful sweet and sour sauce. If this recipe is to be served as a main course, increase the amount of shrimp, clams and pork equally.

Basic

½ pound jumbo shrimp	3 scallions
½ pound clams	4 mushrooms
½ pound lean pork	5 tablespoons cornstarch
1 clove garlic	2 eggs
¼ carrot	1 bottle cooking oil

1. Shell and de-vein the shrimp. Cut them into thirds, leaving the tail attached to the last third. Open the clams (or have them opened by a fish dealer). Cut the pork into squares, roughly equal in size to the shrimp.

2. Slice the garlic and carrot lengthwise. Cut the scallions into 1-inch lengths. Quarter the mushrooms. Combine the vegetables, pork and shellfish in a bowl. Add the cornstarch and mix thoroughly until all sides of the pork and shellfish are coated. Add 2 slightly beaten eggs one at a time and mix well.

3. Heat the cooking oil to 350 degrees and deep fry the fish, meat and vegetables until browned. Drain on a paper towel.

Sweet and Sour Sauce

2 tablespoons vinegar
1 tablespoon soy sauce
1½ tablespoons sugar
1 teaspoon salt

pepper
2 tablespoons cornstarch
⅓ cup cold water

1. Combine the vinegar, soy sauce, sugar, salt
and pepper with the shellfish, pork and vegetables
in a saucepan. Heat.

2. Mix the cornstarch and water. Add this mixture slowly
to the sauce as it comes to a boil. Boil vigorously for
1 minute. Serve piping hot.

Makes 4 servings.

DAEHAP CHUNYUA
CLAMS ON THE HALF SHELL

Sautéed and served in their shells, these clams make
appetizing hors d'oeuvres.

5 clams	½ teaspoon sesame oil
3 scallions	¼ teaspoon salt
1 small clove garlic	dash black pepper
1 ounce chopped beef	1 teaspoon flour
1 ounce chopped pork	2 eggs
¼ teaspoon sesame seeds	1 teaspoon cooking oil

1. Have a fish dealer open the clams. Save the shells.
Clean the clams by pressing out the neck. Cut the clams
into approximately 3 pieces.

2. Mince the scallions and crush the garlic. Combine
these ingredients with the beef, pork, clams, sesame
seeds, sesame oil, salt and pepper in a bowl. Mix in the
flour and eggs.

3. Heat the oil in a frying pan. Add the clam mixture a
tablespoonful at a time. Press the mixture down, then fold
over as for an omelet. Cook until brown and hardened.
If the mixture becomes too brown, cover the pan for a
few minutes and steam. Arrange on the clam shells.

Makes 10 half shells.

Variation: Substitute oysters for clams.

KUL CHIM
OYSTERS STEAMED IN THE SHELL

The combination of meat and fish steamed in oyster shells
provides an unusual and interesting taste treat. This
dish is a welcome addition to a party table or may be
served as an hors d'oeuvre.

5 oysters	½ teaspoon sesame oil
2 ounces ground pork	½ teaspoon salt
2 scallions	dash black pepper
1 small clove garlic	1 egg
¼ teaspoon sesame seeds	10 pine nuts

1. Have a fish dealer open the shells. Lift off the shallow
shells. Loosen the oysters from the shells with the
point of a knife. Reserve the shells.

2. Leave the oysters whole if small, or chop into 3 pieces
if large. Mince the scallions and crush the garlic. Mix
both ingredients in a bowl with the ground meat,
sesame seed, sesame oil, salt and pepper.
Add the egg and mix thoroughly.

3. Place a teaspoonful of the mixture on the deep half of each shell. Decorate with 2 pine nuts and cover with the top shells. Steam on a rack in a pot with a tight-fitting lid or in a steamer for 15 minutes.

Makes 5 oysters.

Variations: Substitute clams (preferably, soft-shelled) for oysters.

Substitute chicken for the ground pork.

KWAE BOKUM
BLUE CRABS

Cooked in their shells, blue crabs are not the easiest
shellfish to eat. The meat must be picked out at the table.
But as any fancier of this shellfish would admit, the
rewards far outweigh the effort.

8 live blue crabs	1 tablespoon sesame oil
2 cloves garlic	1 teaspoon salt
2 scallions	1 cup cold water

1. Have a fish dealer cut the live crabs in the following
manner: Remove the back shell and the innards. Halve
the crab down the center, leaving the claws attached
to the body.

2. Slice the garlic. Cut the scallions into 1½-inch lengths.

3. Heat the sesame oil in a heavy pot. Sauté the crabs,
scallions and garlic for 2 minutes. Add the water and salt
and cover. Steam for 15 minutes. Adjust the flame and
watch the water level in the pot carefully. If too much
water remains when the steaming is complete, the flavor
will be lost. If there is not enough water left,
the crabs will burn.

Makes 2 to 4 servings.

KWAE CHORIM
BLUE CRABS IN SOY SAUCE

The fingers must be used to eat blue crabs. Cooked in soy
sauce that darkens the crab shells and seasoned with
hot peppers, this side dish is spicy fare. Yet the crab meat
itself retains a pure and delicate flavor.

5 blue crabs
5 scallions
2 cloves garlic
¼ pound chopped meat
⅓ cup beef broth
⅓ cup soy sauce

1 tablespoon sesame oil
1 tablespoon sesame
  seeds
1 teaspoon hot red
  peppers, crushed

1. Clean and quarter (or have a fish dealer clean and
quarter) the crabs, then crack the claws.

2. Cut the scallions into 1-inch lengths and slice the garlic
lengthwise. Combine both ingredients in a large saucepan
with the meat, broth, soy sauce, sesame oil, sesame
seeds and red peppers. Add the crabs and cook over
a high flame for 15 minutes. Serve immediately.

Makes 4 servings.

KAZAE
LOBSTER

The whole lobster is cooked in a sauce which lightly
permeates the meat. The taste is delicate, but the manner
of eating is not. Fingers and mallets are recommended.

1 lobster	1 tablespoon white wine
4 cups water	or sherry
3 cloves garlic	1 tablespoon sesame oil
2 scallions	2 tablespoons sugar
1 cup beef broth	dash pepper
1/3 cup soy sauce	

1. Cut (or have a fish dealer cut) the tail of a live lobster
across the body into 3 pieces with the movable joint
in the center of each piece. Split the body shell in half
down the center. Spread the lobster open and remove the
black line and the stomach.

2. Bring the water to a boil, drop in the lobster pieces
and remove them almost immediately. Rinse the pieces
under cold water and drain. Cut off the claws and
crack them.
3. Arrange all the lobster pieces in a saucepan. Slice the
garlic, chop the scallions and add them to the lobster
along with the remaining ingredients. Bring to a boil and
cook for 20 minutes.

Makes 2 to 4 servings.

TWIKIM WANJA
ASSORTED APPETIZERS—DEEP FRIED

Korean meals do not have first, second and third courses.
However, the following ingredients may be combined
to form an hors d'oeuvres tray.

4 jumbo shrimp

½ pound fresh salmon
    fillets

salt

pepper

1 cake bean curd

4 mushrooms

1 scallion

1 carrot

flour for dredging

¼ cup flour

5 tablespoons water

oil for deep frying

1. Shell and de-vein the shrimp, leaving the tail attached.
Slit the shrimp lengthwise down the back, but do not cut
all the way through the flesh. Flatten the shrimp and
cut the fillets in 4 pieces. Sprinkle both the shrimp
and the fillets with salt and pepper.

2. Cut the bean cake into 6 pieces. Halve the mushrooms.
Cut the scallion into 4 pieces, then make slits down 3
sides. Halve the carrot, then cut each half into 4
pieces and make slits down the sides.

3. Dredge the shrimp, fillets, mushrooms, scallions and
carrots in the flour.

4. Mix ¼ cup flour and water until it has the consistency
of pancake batter. Heat the oil to 400 degrees. Dip
the fish and vegetables into the batter and deep fry for
4 minutes or until golden.

Makes 4 servings.

Variations: Substitute prawns for shrimp. Substitute
tuna for salmon.

SAENGSUN BUCHIM
FISH SAUTE

A single fish or a combination of several fish may be used
in this simple recipe. Fresh tuna and salmon are
particularly delectable.

1 pound fresh salmon	3 tablespoons sesame or
salt	salad oil
pepper	2 eggs
flour for dredging	¼ cup soy sauce

1. Cut the salmon into 2-inch lengths. Sprinkle with salt
and pepper, then dredge in flour.

2. Heat a small amount of the sesame oil in a heavy-
bottomed frying pan. Beat the eggs slightly. Dip the
salmon into the beaten eggs, then sauté it in oil for about
4 minutes or until golden. Add oil as needed.

3. Serve with a side dish of soy sauce for dipping.

Makes 4 servings.

Variations: Tuna, sole or flounder may be substituted
for the salmon or used in any combination.

SAENGSUN CHUNYUA
FISH FRIED IN EGG BATTER

Chunyua describes a number of Korean dishes which are
coated with egg before frying. This particular recipe
can be made with any good fish fillet, or several varieties
may be combined to obtain subtle taste differences
without complicating the preparation.

½ pound red snapper   3 tablespoons flour
   fillets   2 eggs
½ teaspoon salt   ⅓ cup sesame oil
black pepper

1. Slice the fillets across the grain into 4 or 5 pieces. Cut
them in half down the back to make bite-sized pieces. If
shrimp are used, shell and de-vein them. Slit them down
the back, being careful not to cut all the way through.
Flatten the shrimp with the broad side of a knife and
score them lightly. Sprinkle the pieces with salt and black
pepper. Dredge them in flour.

2. Heat the oil in a heavy frying pan until very hot. Beat the eggs slightly in a bowl. Dip the fish into the eggs and sauté. A minute on each side should be sufficient time to brown the fish. Turn off the heat and let the fillets cook a few more minutes in the hot pan. Serve immediately.

Makes 2 servings.

Variations: Substitute any of the following for the red snapper: jumbo shrimp, flounder, salmon, tuna or sole.

SAENGSUN SANJUK CHUNYUA
SOLE SHISH KEBAB

This shish kebab recipe comprises fish and vegetables
arranged on skewers, which are dipped in egg and
sautéed. The mixture of the flavors is unusual
and rather delicate.

½ carrot
5 scallions
½ pound sole
2 cloves garlic
½ teaspoon sesame oil
1 teaspoon sesame seeds

¾ teaspoon salt
dash black pepper
2 eggs
3 tablespoons flour
⅓ cup sesame oil

1. Quarter the carrot lengthwise, then cut each quarter
into 2-inch lengths. Slice the scallions into 2-inch
lengths. Cut the fish into pieces about 1 inch wide and
2½ inches long. (The fish will shrink slightly during
cooking.) Place the fish and vegetables in a bowl. Crush
the garlic and add it, the sesame oil, sesame seeds,
salt and pepper to the fish. Mix well.

2. Beat the eggs slightly in a bowl. Alternate a scallion,
a piece of fish and a carrot on a wooden skewer or on a
wooden toothpick. Dredge the skewers in flour, then
dip them into the eggs.

3. Heat the oil in a heavy frying pan until very hot. Saute the skewers until browned. The fish must be cooked a little longer than usual to allow the carrot and scallion to become slightly tender. Total cooking time is about 5 minutes or until the shish kebab turns a dark golden brown. Arrange on a platter and serve immediately.

Makes 2 to 4 servings: 12 small wooden skewers.

Variations: Substitute any of the following for the sole: red snapper, flounder, salmon, tuna or shrimp. When using shrimp, make sure that the underside of the shrimp is fried first, and the outside or back last. This sequence will prevent the back from curling up.

DOMI CHIM
STEAMED RED SNAPPER

The steaming process does not alter the brilliant color of
the red snapper. This fish recipe is easy and quick
to prepare; the sauce adds the proper zest.

1 red snapper (about 2 pounds)	2 large button mushrooms
1 lemon	2 tablespoons white wine or rice wine

1. Have the fish cleaned, leaving the head and tail intact.
Make a deep cut down the center of the fish, then five
crosswise cuts. Turn the fish over and repeat
the same process.

2. Place the fish on the rack of a fish steamer, or on a
platter raised above water in a roasting pan. If a lid
is not available, aluminum foil may be substituted. The
pan must be tightly covered. Arrange thin slices of
lemon on top of the fish and mushroom quarters around
its edges. Sprinkle with white wine. Cover and steam for
about 20 minutes or until the fish flakes easily.
Serve with steamed red snapper sauce.

Makes 2 to 4 servings.

CHANG
STEAMED RED SNAPPER SAUCE

Steamed red snapper sauce should not be too tart or too bland. Since vinegar varies in strength, add gradually until satisfied with the taste of this fish sauce.

2 cloves garlic
4 scallions
½ cup soy sauce
1 tablespoon sesame
  seeds
1 tablespoon sesame oil

1 tablespoon sugar
1 teaspoon red pepper,
  crushed
1 cup beef broth
vinegar to taste
1 small lemon

1. Crush the garlic and chop the scallions fine. Mix together the garlic, scallions, soy sauce, sesame seeds, sesame oil, sugar and red pepper. Add the broth and vinegar slowly.

2. In small individual bowls serve the sauce and a thin lemon slice if desired.

Makes 2 servings.

DOMI
RED SNAPPER

Red snapper is filleted, then "reconstructed" using a combination of fish and meat which is as pleasing to the palate as it is unusual to the eye.

1 medium red snapper	dash salt
flour for dredging	dash pepper
1 clove garlic	sesame or salad oil
½ cup ground beef	3 eggs
½ teaspoon sesame oil	¼ red bell pepper

1. Have the fish filleted, retaining the carcass in one piece. Cut the fish fillets into 8 pieces for serving. Dredge them in flour.

2. Crush the garlic and combine it with the ground beef, ½ teaspoon sesame oil, salt and pepper in a bowl. Flatten the beef into a 4-inch pancake, then cut it in half. Dredge the meat in flour.

3. Heat a small amount of sesame oil in a large frying pan. Beat the eggs in a bowl. Dip the fillets into the eggs, then sauté until golden on both sides or for about 4 minutes. Set aside. Dredge the fish carcass in flour, then dip it into the eggs. Sauté the carcass in a small amount of heated oil in the same manner and set aside.

4. Dip the ground beef patty into the eggs and fry on both sides in the same pan used for the fish. Cut the meat into 8 pieces.

5. Place the fish carcass on a serving platter. Alternate the fish and meat wedges on the carcass to reconstruct the original fish shape. Decorate with 4 strips red bell pepper. To reheat and combine flavors, steam over a pan of boiling water for 4 minutes and serve.

Makes 2 servings.

HUK DOMI
SEA BASS

Sauce

¼ carrot	1 tablespoon oil
1 leaf Chinese cabbage	1 cup beef stock
1 scallion	2 tablespoons soy sauce
1 clove garlic	2 teaspoons cornstarch
2 mushrooms	½ cup cold water
¼ medium-sized onion	dash black pepper
2 thin slices hot red or green pepper	

Sauce

1. Slice the carrot paper-thin on a diagonal. Cut the
Chinese cabbage into 1-inch squares. Cut the scallion
into 1½-inch lengths. Slice the garlic.

2. Heat the oil in a skillet until it is very hot. Sauté the
mushrooms, carrot, Chinese cabbage, scallion, onion and
hot pepper until almost crisp. Add the stock slowly,
then add the soy sauce and garlic. Blend the cornstarch
with cold water and add this mixture to the sauce. Season
with pepper. Boil vigorously for 3 minutes. Simmer for
5 additional minutes.

Fish
1 sea bass (about 1½ pounds)
¼ cup cornstarch

3 tablespoons sesame or salad oil
2 eggs
5 gingko nuts

1. Have the fish filleted, retaining the carcass in one piece. Cut the fillets into 8 pieces. Dredge the carcass and fish pieces in the cornstarch.

2. Heat a small amount of oil in a large frying pan. Beat the eggs slightly in a bowl. Dip the fillets into the eggs, then sauté them on both sides for about 3 minutes or until crisp. Heat more oil and dip the fish carcass into the eggs and sauté as for fillets.

3. Arrange the filleted pieces on top of the carcass, reconstructing the fish shape. Pour the sauce over the bass. Decorate with gingko nuts.

Makes 2 servings.

SAENGSUN KOCHU CHANG KUI
GRILLED SOLE IN RED SAUCE

2 fillets of sole (about ¾
   pound)
2 scallions
3 cloves garlic
1 tablespoon kochu
   chang (See page 263)

1 tablespoon sesame oil
1 tablespoon sesame
   seeds
1 tablespoon soy sauce
1 teaspoon sugar
dash black pepper

1. Cut each fillet into 4 pieces. Mince the scallions and crush the garlic.

2. Combine the scallions, garlic, kochu chang, sesame oil, sesame seeds, soy sauce, sugar and pepper in a bowl. Add the fish and mix well until all sides of the sole are coated.

3. Grill. Do not overcook or the sole will fall apart easily and lose its flavor.

Makes 2 to 4 servings.

Variations: Substitute any of the following for the sole: salmon, fresh tuna, red snapper, sea bass or scallops.

UH YUK MU NAMUL
SALT COD WITH CHICKEN AND TURNIP

In Korean cookery meat and fish are often combined, a practice that is rare in the West. Koreans believe that fish flavors a dish and meat gives it body.

½ pound salt cod
2 cups cold water
2 chicken legs (or ¾ pound, preferably a young chicken)

1 pound Chinese turnip
3 cloves garlic
2 tablespoons oil
1 tablespoon soy sauce
dash black pepper

1. Wash the codfish, then slice it into finger-shaped pieces about 2 inches long and ⅓ inch wide. Place the codfish in a saucepan and cover it with the water. Bring to a boil. Continue boiling for 3 minutes, then remove from heat. Do not drain.

2. Chop (or have a butcher chop) each chicken leg in half. If the legs are large, chop them into thirds. Score them deeply on both sides. Slice the turnip into pieces about ⅓ inch wide, then cut these pieces into thirds. Slice the garlic diagonally.

3. Heat the oil in a heavy-bottomed skillet. Brown the garlic slightly. Add the chicken and turnip and brown on both sides over a high flame for about 5 minutes. Add the soy sauce and sauté for 2 minutes longer. Add the codfish and 1 cup water from the fish. Cover and simmer for 20 minutes. Season with pepper.

Makes 4 servings.

GODUNG-UH CHORIM
MACKEREL STEW

This stew is a dark, pungent, soy-sauce-like dish. It does
not have an oily mackerel taste. Its flavor may be
too piquant for a main dish. Try the recipe in small
quantities first. Beware, bones are included!

1 mackerel
4 cups water
3 cloves garlic
2 scallions, including
   green stems
½ cup soy sauce
1 tablespoon wine or
   sherry
½ cup beef broth

1 teaspoon sesame seeds
1 teaspoon sesame oil
2 teaspoons sugar
1 teaspoon red pepper,
   crushed
dash black pepper
dash thread red pepper
   (optional)

1. Have the fish cleaned and its head and tail removed.
Slice the fish across the body into 1¼-inch pieces or into
approximately 8 pieces.

2. Bring the water to a boil. Drop the mackerel into the
water and remove it immediately. Rinse under cold water
and drain. This procedure will eliminate any fish smell,
and any impurities inside the mackerel.

3. Slice the garlic, chop the scallions, and combine them with all the other ingredients for the sauce in a large bowl. Place the mackerel in a pan, pour the sauce ingredients over it and bring to a boil. Cooking time should not exceed 10 minutes.

Makes 4 servings.

YUPKOL CHO
SHARK'S FINS

Expensive to buy and time-consuming to prepare, shark's
fins are served on festive occasions. Resembling strings
of golden vermicelli glued together, they are sold
dried and will keep indefinitely.

¼ pound shark's fins
8 cups water
oil for frying
½ pound chicken breasts,
  boned
2 tablespoons potato
  starch
2 cups water
3 whole red peppers,
  fresh or dried
1 tablespoon soy sauce
2 tablespoons sugar
2 tablespoons vinegar
½ teaspoon salt
¼ pound lean pork
¼ pound flank steak
2 tablespoons potato
  starch

4 cups water
2 cloves garlic
2 scallions
1 cup cloud-ear
  mushrooms
1 cup cut Chinese
  cabbage
2 inches carrot
2 button mushrooms
2 cups beef stock
1½ tablespoons potato
  starch
⅓ cup beef stock
¼ cup soy sauce
dash black pepper
10 pine nuts
egg decoration

1. Soak the shark's fins in warm water for 3 hours. To
separate the fins, rub them together gently. Remove any
hard bits. Drain. Soak the cloud-ear mushrooms.

2. Heat the oil for deep frying in a pan to 400 degrees. Flatten out the chicken breast, and then score it lightly on both sides. Dredge the breast in the potato starch, then fry it in the hot oil until browned. Place the chicken in 2 cups cold water with the red peppers and bring to a boil. Add the soy sauce, sugar, vinegar and salt. Boil for 15 minutes. Reserve the broth.

3. While the chicken is cooking, slice the pork thin on the bias, then again across the grain into fine strips. Slice the beef in the same manner. Dredge the beef and the pork strips in the potato starch, separating the pieces to make certain that all sides of the meat are coated. Bring 4 cups water to a boil. Drop the beef and pork strips into the boiling water. Bring to a second boil, then boil an additional minute. Drain and rinse the meat under cold running water. (The meat will be shiny, slippery and soft.)

4. Slice the garlic into thin slivers. Cut the scallions into 1½-inch lengths, then cut them into slivers. Slice the cloud-ear mushrooms into thin slivers. Cut the Chinese cabbage into 1½-inch lengths, then into thin finger-shaped pieces. Slice the carrot into slivers. Halve the button mushrooms.

5. Heat the 2 cups of stock in a large frying pan. Add the garlic, scallions, Chinese cabbage, carrot, the two kinds of mushrooms and the broth from the chicken. Cook over a high flame until the vegetables are just barely tender. Combine the potato starch and the remaining ⅓ cup stock. Add the soy sauce and pepper to the vegetables, then add the starch mixture. The sauce should have the consistency of a very light gravy. If it needs to be thinned, add a little more stock.

6. Slice the chicken thin on the bias and arrange it on the bottom of a serving platter. Place the shark's fins on the chicken, then add the beef and pork. Arrange the vegetables in the sauce on top of the meat. Sprinkle with pine nuts and egg decoration. Serve immediately.

Makes 4 to 8 servings.

UH CHAE
CONCHS

Conchs may be purchased in larger cities either in
Chinese or Greek or Italian markets. Or a local fish dealer
may be able to supply them on order.

5 very large conchs   4 cups cold water

1. Place the conchs in the water. Bring the water to a boil.
Continue boiling vigorously for an additional 10 minutes.

2. Drain the water and remove the conchs from their
shells. Slice the conchs down the center and remove the
innards under cold running water.

3. Serve cold with the kochu chang sauce suggested for
squid (See page 167).

Makes 5 servings.

OZING-UH CHAE
COOKED SQUID

Squid, believe it or not, is served as a matter of course in
Korea—like American peanuts! Cooked squid is tastier
and more tender than raw squid. Do not overcook,
for while a moment's boiling softens the squid, additional
cooking time toughens it. One pound of squid is
needed to obtain ½ pound of cleaned squid.

½ pound cleaned squid   2 cups water

1. Clean the squid. (See the directions for raw squid, the
next recipe.) Slice it lengthwise into strips 1½ inches
wide. Score the squid on one side then slice again
diagonally into strips 1 inch wide. This way of
cutting prevents shrinkage when boiling.

2. Bring the water to a boil. Add the squid. Allow it to
boil for no longer than 30 seconds, drain and rinse under
cold water.

3. Arrange on a bed of lettuce and serve with kochu
chang sauce (See page 263).

Makes 4 servings.

OZING-UH WHE
RAW SQUID

Raw squid is an appetizer for the adventuresome. It does not have a strong taste and is only slightly chewy.

1 pound uncleaned squid   ½ pound cleaned squid
  or

1. To clean squid, pull out the head and the tentacles, then cut down the center of the back. Remove the inner membrane and the outside skin under running water. The skin peels off easily. Trim the long ends off the tentacles and cut off the head just above the tentacles. The head may also be eaten, but the ink must be removed and this is a delicate operation, best left to the proficient.

2. Slice the squid into very thin strips about 1½ inches long across the grain. Arrange the strips on a bed of lettuce leaves and serve with kochu chang sauce. (See specific recipe)

Makes 4 to 6 servings.

KOCHU CHANG SAUCE FOR SQUID

This sauce, slightly piquant but not really hot, has a lovely red color. The measurements given will provide sauce for one pound of cleaned squid, cooked or raw.

2 cloves garlic
1 scallion
⅓ cup kochu chang
   (See page 263)
1 tablespoon vinegar

1 tablespoon soy sauce
1 tablespoon sesame oil
1 tablespoon sesame
   seeds
2 tablespoons sugar

1. Crush the garlic. Chop the scallion fine. Mix all the ingredients together.

2. Serve in 2 or more small bowls.

OZING-UH
DRIED SQUID

1 cup dried squid strips, soaked

1. Soak the squid strips in hot water for 30 minutes. Change the water and soak for an additional 30 minutes. Drain and cut into 1½-inch lengths.

Sauce
1 clove garlic
1 scallion
1 teaspoon vinegar
1 teaspoon sugar

2 tablespoons kochu chang (See page 263)
½ teaspoon sesame oil

1. Crush the garlic, mince the scallion and mix well with the vinegar, sugar, kochu chang and sesame oil. Add the squid to the sauce and mix thoroughly.

Makes 4 servings.

BAENG-UH PO BOKUM
DRIED WHITEBAIT

Strong-tasting and rather salty, dried whitebait is a
delicacy in which Koreans, especially those from the
South, delight. As a side dish, it may accompany any
Korean meal. It will keep for weeks or even
months in a refrigerator.

⅓ cup cooking oil	1¼ cup soy sauce
1-pound bag of tiny	1 cup beef stock
whole whitebait	2 tablespoons hot
3 scallions	cayenne pepper
2 cloves garlic	⅓ cup sugar

1. Heat the oil in a large skillet. Add the whitebait and
stir gently in the oil. Sauté for about 5 minutes.

2. Mince the scallions and garlic and add them to the
whitebait. Add the soy sauce, stock, cayenne pepper and
sugar. Mix all the ingredients well. Continue cooking
for 15 minutes longer.

3. Refrigerate in a jar.

Makes about 30 servings.

KIM
SEAWEED: THIN LAVER

This dark purple, paper-thin seaweed appears almost black. As a side dish, laver is often wrapped around some rice with one of the kochu chang sauces added to heighten the flavor, or, wrapped around some rice and vegetables, it is another staple of the picnic and the lunch box.

12 sheets thin laver   salt
4 tablespoons sesame oil

1. Separate the pieces of laver. Pour a small amount of the sesame oil into a dish, then lightly brush both sides of the laver with the oil. Sprinkle salt on each sheet.

2. Heat the oven grill. Place the sheets of laver one at a time under the grill for about 10 seconds. The laver should be crisp but not burnt. (It will only become crisp after it has cooled for an instant.)

3. Pile the laver sheets, then cut them into quarters. Place the quartered pieces in a mound and spear each with a toothpick.

Makes 4 servings.

VEGETABLES

SIGUMCHI NAMUL
SPINACH

1 pound fresh spinach
3 tablespoons soy sauce
2 tablespoons sesame oil
1 tablespoon sesame
   seeds

1 clove garlic, crushed
1 tablespoon sugar
1 tablespoon white
   vinegar
dash pepper

1. Wash the spinach. Steam until just tender and still green. Strain and squeeze out as much water as possible. Cut spinach very coarsely.

2. Combine the soy sauce, sesame oil, sesame seeds, garlic, sugar, vinegar and pepper. Mix into the spinach.

Variation: Season the spinach with the meat sauce for vegetables. (See page 179).

OI NAMUL
CUCUMBER VEGETABLE

This simple cucumber salad is a pleasant accompaniment to a hot summer night. Small cucumbers are suggested; they are not quite as watery as the large ones nor do they require peeling.

3 cucumbers
1 tablespoon salt
1 clove garlic
¼ teaspoon salt
1 teaspoon sesame seeds

1 teaspoon sesame oil
¼ teaspoon cayenne
   pepper
1 teaspoon sugar

1. Slice the cucumbers in circles. Sprinkle salt over the cucumber slices, mix well and let them stand for 30 minutes. Place the cucumbers in a damp cloth and gently but firmly squeeze out as much water as possible. The less watery the cucumbers, the better tasting the dish.

2. Crush the garlic, then combine it with the cucumbers, salt, sesame seeds, sesame oil, pepper and sugar in a bowl. Mix well.

Makes 4 servings.

KONG NAMUL
YELLOW BEAN SPROUTS

1 pound bean sprouts   1 tablespoon sugar
¼ cup water   2 tablespoons meat sauce
2 tablespoons sesame oil   (See page 179)
1 teaspoon salt

1. Wash the bean sprouts. Place them in a pot with water
and bring slowly to a boil. Place a tight-fitting lid on
the pot and steam for 10 minutes. Drain immediately.

2. Heat the sesame oil in a skillet. Sauté the bean sprouts
in the oil. Season them with salt and sugar after 1
minute. Add the meat sauce and cook until heated. Blend
the flavors and serve.

Makes 4 servings.

HO BAECHU
CABBAGE

6 leaves Chinese cabbage
1 clove garlic
1 tablespoon sesame oil
½ teaspoon sesame seeds

dash cayenne pepper
dash black pepper
2 tablespoons meat sauce
 (See page 179)

1. Shred the cabbage into thin strips and steam until just tender. After cooking, there should be 2 cups of cabbage remaining.

2. Crush the garlic, then add it, the sesame oil, sesame seeds, the cayenne and black pepper to the cabbage. Add the meat sauce. Cook over a high flame for 2 minutes to blend the flavors.

Makes 4 servings.

KOSARI
ROYAL FERN VEGETABLE

Almost one thousand years before the birth of Christ, a
minister of the Chinese court of Chou disagreed with the
emperor on a matter of policy. He left the court and
took refuge in the mountains, swearing that never again
would he touch anything belonging to the Emperor.
He drank only fresh water and ate ferns.

Since ancient times, these ferns have had a symbolic value
of integrity and purity. Buddhist monks who cannot
partake of meat still eat these ferns today. They are so
nutritious that they replace meat in the diet of these
mountain hermits.

The young shoots when they first come up in the spring
are picked and dried, and can be stored indefinitely.

½ package royal ferns
2 cloves garlic
1 tablespoon sesame oil
1 teaspoon sesame seeds

pepper to taste
2 tablespoons meat sauce
 (See page 179)

1. Soak the royal ferns in hot water overnight. Drain.
Place them in a pot and cover with water. Bring the
water to a boil. Boil 1 minute longer and drain. Remove
any hard ends, then cut the ferns into 1½-inch lengths.

2. Crush the garlic, then add it, the sesame oil, sesame seeds and pepper to the ferns. Add the meat sauce. Boil until all the liquid has evaporated. Serve warm or cool, but not chilled.

Makes 4 servings.

CHANG
MEAT SAUCE FOR VEGETABLES

This meat sauce can be made in advance and stored in
large quantities in the refrigerator. It will keep
indefinitely. Use about 2 tablespoons per pound of
vegetables or 1 tablespoon per cup of cooked vegetables.

6 cloves garlic
1 tablespoon sesame oil
1 pound ground round
    steak

1 cup soy sauce
1 cup soup stock

1. Crush the garlic. Heat the sesame oil in a large frying
pan. Brown the meat and garlic in the sesame oil,
stirring constantly for 10 minutes. Add the soy sauce
and soup stock. Simmer, uncovered, for 10 minutes.

2. When the sauce has cooled, skim off the fat and store
for use as desired.

TUBU BOKUM
BEAN CURD SAUTÉ

2 cakes bean curd
pinch salt
pinch pepper

1 tablespoon sesame oil
flour for dredging
1 egg, slightly beaten

1. Cut each bean curd into about 6 pieces and sprinkle with salt and pepper.

2. Heat the oil in a frying pan. Dredge the bean curd in flour, then dip them into a beaten egg and sauté for about 4 minutes or until golden on both sides.

Makes 4 servings.

YACHAE SANJUK CHUNYUA
VEGETABLES ON A SKEWER

12 mushrooms
¾ teaspoon salt
1 carrot
12 scallions
black pepper
½ teaspoon sesame oil

1 teaspoon sesame seeds
2 cloves garlic
3 tablespoons flour
2 eggs
⅓ cup sesame oil

1. Halve the mushrooms and sprinkle with salt. If the mushrooms are set aside for an hour, the stems will not break off when they are placed on the skewers. Cut the carrot into 2-inch lengths, then quarter each piece. There should be 12 carrot slices. Cut 2 two-inch lengths from the white end of the scallions. Mix together the mushrooms, carrot slices and scallions in a bowl. Season them with pepper, sesame oil, sesame seeds and garlic. Mix well and arrange on skewers in the following order: Scallion. Mushroom. Carrot. Mushroom. Scallion.

2. Beat the eggs slightly in a bowl. Dredge the skewers in flour, then dip them into the beaten eggs. Heat ⅓ cup sesame oil in a pan. Sauté the skewers in a very hot pan until browned, and the carrot and scallion are just tender. Cooking time is about 5 minutes. Arrange the skewers on a platter and serve immediately.

Makes 4 to 6 servings: 12 wooden skewers or toothpicks.

YACHAE SANJUK
SKEWERED ASPARAGUS

¼ pound asparagus   1 teaspoon sesame oil
  (about 12 stalks)   1 teaspoon sesame seeds
¼ pound lean pork   ½ teaspoon salt
1 clove garlic   dash black pepper

1. Remove the hard ends of the asparagus. Parboil for 5 minutes or until crunchy but edible. Drain and set aside.

2. Slice the pork into pieces 3 inches long and ½ inch wide.

3. Crush the garlic and combine with the sesame oil, sesame seeds, salt and pepper in a bowl. Add the asparagus and pork strips and mix well until all sides of the pork are coated. Arrange the meat and asparagus alternately on small skewers.

4. Grill until the pork is well done.

Makes 4 skewers.

Variation: Substitute beef for pork.

Stuffed Eggplant (*Kaji Chim,* see p. 191)

Cucumber with Pork (*Oi Bokum,* see p. 201)

Nine-Course Hors D'oeuvre Tray (*Kujol Pan,* see p. 216)

Turnip Salad (*Mu Sangchae,* see p. 236)

Stuffed Kimchi (*Sobaegi Kimchi,* see p. 243)

Rice with Yellow Bean Sprouts(*Kongnamul Bab,* see p. 253)

Korean Cakes(*Yak Kwa,* see p. 272)

Ginseng Cake (*Insam Chunkwa*, see p. 274)

Medicinal Cake (*Yak Sik*, see p. 275)

Ingredients I

mustard sauce (*keja*)

salt (*sogum*)

red bean paste (*kochu chang*)

sesame seeds (*kkaesogum*)

soy sauce (*kanjang*)

cooking oil (*shigyongyu*)

brown bean paste (*daenchang*)

sesame oil (*chamgirum*)

Ingredients II

1. Chinese turnip (*mu*)
2. carrot (*tanggun*)
3. potato (*kamja*)
4. parsely (*pasulli*)
5. lettuce (*sangchi*)
6. onion (*yangpa*)
7. green pepper (*putkochu*)
8. red pepper (*pulgun kochu*)
9. *minari*
10. bean sprout (*kongnamul*)
11. zucchini (*hobak*)
12. eggplant (*kaji*)
13. ginseng (*insam*)
14. dried persimmon (*kotkam*)
15. chestnut (*pam*)
16. jujubes (*taechu*)
17. cayenne pepper (*kochu karu*)
18. pine mushroom (*songi posot*)
19. ginger (*saenggang*)
20. garlic (*manul*)
21. egg (*kyeran*)

YACHAE CHUNYUA
SKEWERED ASPARAGUS FRIED IN EGG BATTER

¼ pound asparagus
(about 12 stalks)
¼ pound lean pork
1 clove garlic
1 teaspoon sesame oil
1 teaspoon sesame seeds

½ teaspoon salt
dash black pepper
2 tablespoons flour
2 eggs
2 teaspoons cooking oil

1. Remove the hard ends from the asparagus. Parboil the asparagus for 5 minutes to soften. Drain and set aside.

2. Slice the pork into pieces 3 inches long and about ½ inch wide.

3. Crush the garlic and combine with the sesame oil, sesame seeds, salt and pepper in a bowl. Add the asparagus stalks and pork strips and mix well until all sides of the pork are coated. Arrange the meat and asparagus alternately on small skewers.

4. Sprinkle the flour over the skewers, coating both sides. Beat the eggs slightly in a bowl.

5. Heat the oil in a frying pan. When the oil is very hot, dip the skewers into the eggs, then fry until well browned on both sides. The skewers are cooked when the asparagus can easily be pierced with a chopstick or a fork. The stalks should be crunchy, not soft.

Makes 4 skewers.

WANDU KONG
SKEWERED STRING BEANS

½ pound lean pork
24 string beans
1 clove garlic
1 tablespoon sesame oil

1 teaspoon sesame seeds
½ teaspoon salt
dash black pepper

1. Slice the pork into strips 3 inches long and about ½ inch wide. Cut the string beans into 3-inch lengths.

2. Crush the garlic and combine with the sesame oil, sesame seeds, salt and pepper. Add the beans and pork and mix well until all sides of the pork and beans are coated.

3. Arrange the pork and beans on skewers. Alternate 2 string beans with a slice of pork. Use 3 slices of pork per skewer.

4. Grill. The pork should be well done.

Makes 3 skewers.

WANDU KONG CHUNYUA
SKEWERED STRING BEANS FRIED IN EGG BATTER

½ pound lean pork
24 string beans
1 clove garlic
1 tablespoon sesame oil
1 teaspoon sesame seeds

½ teaspoon salt
dash black pepper
2 tablespoons flour
2 eggs
2 teaspoons cooking oil

1. Slice the pork into strips 3 inches long and about ½ inch wide. Cut the string beans into 3-inch lengths.

2. Crush the garlic and combine with the sesame oil, sesame seeds, salt and pepper in a bowl. Add the beans and pork and mix well until all sides of the pork are coated.

3. Alternate 2 string beans with one strip of pork on the skewers. Use 3 pork strips per skewer.

4. Sprinkle the flour over the skewers, coating both sides. Beat the eggs slightly in a bowl.

5. Heat the oil in a frying pan. When the oil is very hot, dip the skewers into the eggs, then fry until well browned on both sides. The skewers are cooked when the beans can easily be pierced with a chopstick or a fork. The beans should be crunchy, not soft.

Makes 3 skewers.

CHANG
SAUCE FOR STUFFED VEGETABLES

This sauce has the texture of light brown gravy; its taste is mild. The following proportions are for 1 cup liquid. If several steamed vegetables are made, ingredients for the sauce should be increased proportionately.

1 scallion
1 button mushroom
1 inch of a carrot
1 cup liquid from
   steaming stuffed
   vegetables

1 teaspoon sesame oil
1 tablespoon soy sauce
½ teaspoon salt
1 teaspoon potato starch
   in ¼ cup beef broth
egg decoration

1. Chop the scallion, slice the mushroom and shred the carrot into match-shaped pieces.

2. Bring the liquid to a boil in a pot and add the scallion, mushroom and carrot. Cook for a few minutes, then add the sesame oil, soy sauce and salt. Add the potato starch diluted in the broth. Do not cook after adding the starch.

3. Pour the sauce over the vegetables and decorate with yellow egg strips.

KOCHU CHIM
STUFFED GREEN PEPPERS

The rich stuffing for the green peppers is almost a
meal in itself.

2 large green peppers	1 teaspoon sesame oil
1 heaping tablespoon chopped onion	¼ teaspoon salt
	1 teaspoon sugar
2 cloves garlic	dash black pepper
¼ pound ground beef	1 egg, slightly beaten
¼ pound ground pork	2 teaspoons potato starch
1 teaspoon sesame seeds	egg decoration

1. Remove the stem and seeds from the peppers, leaving
them whole. Soften the peppers by steaming them for
5 minutes over a small amount of boiling water.

2. Chop the onion, crush the garlic and mix all the
ingredients for the stuffing, except for the potato starch,
in a bowl.

Add the beaten egg last. Coat the inside of each pepper
with 1 teaspoon potato starch and add one half of the
stuffing mixture to each pepper. Steam on a rack for 45
minutes or until the meat is completely cooked and
the pepper is tender. Reserve the liquid from
steaming for the sauce.

3. Slice the peppers crosswise, about 3 slices per pepper. Top with *chang,* or the sauce for stuffed vegetables (see page 186), and yellow egg decoration.

Makes 2 to 4 servings.

YANG BAECHU CHIM
STUFFED CABBAGE

Combine the stuffed cabbage, stuffed eggplant and/or the
stuffed green pepper recipes if preparing a dinner for
several people. Since the stuffing for these recipes is the
same, it can be made in one large batch. Only the
preparation and cooking times of the vegetables differ.
Guests will be impressed with the varied menu, which
requires a minimum of cost and effort.

1 small American cabbage	1 teaspoon sesame oil
1 heaping tablespoon	1 teaspoon sugar
chopped onion	¼ teaspoon salt
2 cloves garlic	dash black pepper
½ pound ground beef	1 egg, slightly beaten
¼ pound ground pork	1 teaspoon potato starch
1 teaspoon sesame seeds	

1. Remove the tough center of the cabbage. Bring a few
cups water to a boil in a large pot. Place the cabbage
in the boiling water and cook for 10 minutes. Rinse under
cold running water, then drain off the excess water.
The cabbage will now be pliant.

2. Chop the onion, crush the garlic and combine with all the remaining ingredients, except for the potato starch, in a bowl. Add the egg last. Coat the inside hollow of the cabbage with potato starch, then add the stuffing mixture. The starch will hold the stuffing firmly inside the cabbage as it is cooked, sliced and served.

3: Steam the stuffed cabbage for about 1 hour or until tender. Reserve the liquid from steaming for the sauce. Quarter the cabbage lengthwise and serve with the sauce for stuffed vegetables, *chang* (see page 186).

Makes 2 to 4 servings.

KAJI CHIM
STUFFED EGGPLANT

Stuffed eggplant is a mild-tasting dish served with a delicious sauce.

1 eggplant (about 1 pound)	1 teaspoon sesame seeds
	1 teaspoon sesame oil
¼ pound ground beef	1 teaspoon sugar
¼ pound ground pork	¼ teaspoon salt
1 heaping tablespoon chopped onion	dash black pepper
	1 egg, slightly beaten
2 cloves garlic	1 teaspoon potato starch

1. Hollow out the large end of an eggplant. A portion of the top may be cut off if the eggplant is too large. Leave ½-inch of flesh all around.

2. Place the hollow side face down and soften by steaming over a small amount of water for 6 minutes.

3. In a bowl mix all the ingredients for the stuffing, except for the potato starch. Add the beaten egg last. Coat the inside of the eggplant with the potato starch. Add the stuffing and steam on a rack for about 1 hour or until the meat is thoroughly cooked. Reserve the liquid from steaming for the sauce.

4. Quarter the eggplant lengthwise and serve with the sauce for stuffed vegetables, *chang* (see page 186).

Makes 2 to 4 servings.

SANPA ALSSAM
OMELET WITH CHIVES

This omelet may be eaten warm or prepared in advance
and served cold hours later.

12 chive stalks   1 teaspoon soy sauce
dash salt   ½ teaspoon sugar
dash pepper   1 tablespoon water
6 eggs   sesame oil
¼ teaspoon salt

1. Cook the chives in boiling water for 5 minutes. Drain
and season with salt and pepper.

2. Beat the eggs together with the salt, soy sauce, sugar
and water in a bowl. Place a small amount of oil in
the bottom of a large omelet pan. Add enough egg
mixture to barely cover the bottom of the pan. Stir at the
center for a moment, as for scrambling. Allow to set.
Place the chives in a pile on one side of the omelet. Roll
the omelet over the chives. Allow to cook slowly. Oil
the pan again. Add more eggs. When the eggs have set,
wrap them around the first omelet roll. Repeat this
process until all the egg mixture has been used.

3. Place the omelet on a plate. Roll the ends of the omelet together. Allow to cool and harden, then cut into 1-inch circles for serving.

Makes 6 servings.

SOGOGI PUCHOU BOKUM
BEEF WITH CHINESE CHIVES

Beef with Chinese chives is a good company dish: it
may be prepared in advance, covered and set aside for
several hours without losing its flavor.

½ pound flank steak
2 large hot red peppers
2 tablespoons sesame oil
½ pound Chinese chives

¼ cup soy sauce
1 heaping tablespoon
   sesame seeds

1. Cut the meat across the grain, then shred into
match-shaped pieces 2 inches long. Seed the peppers,
making a cut down one side. Open the peppers flat and
shred them across the grain.

2. Heat the sesame oil in a heavy skillet. Brown the beef
strips quickly. Add the Chinese chives and turn over
several times so that the oil coats all sides. Add the
peppers. When the chives wilt, add the soy sauce
and remove immediately from heat.

3. Mix well with the sesame seeds.

Makes 2 to 4 servings.

Variations: Use sirloin steak instead of flank steak. If a
milder flavor is desired, substitute red bell peppers
for the hot peppers.

SANJUK CHUNYUA

BEEF IN ONION RINGS

Stuffed onions are a good side dish or may be served as
an appetizer. The onions are sliced and their centers
removed and stuffed with seasoned meat.

3 medium onions
¼ teaspoon salt
1 scallion
2 cloves garlic
¼ pound ground beef
2-inch slice of bean curd
   (2 ounces)

½ teaspoon salt
½ teaspoon sesame seeds
½ teaspoon sesame oil
pinch black pepper
3 tablespoons flour
2 eggs
⅓ cup sesame oil

1. Peel, then slice the onions into ½-inch circles.
Remove the centers of the onion rings. Sprinkle the
rounds with salt.

2. Mince the scallion and crush the garlic. Combine these
ingredients with the beef, bean curd, salt, sesame seeds,
sesame oil and pepper in a bowl. Mix well.

3. Dip the onion rings into the flour. Pat the meat
mixture into the center and on the top of the onion rings.
The meat mixture should cover one side of each ring.
Dip the rings into the flour. Beat the eggs slightly in a
bowl. Dip the rings into the eggs.

4. Heat the oil in a skillet. Sauté the onion rings meat-side down until browned, then turn them over. Reduce the heat and cook for about 5 minutes or until the onions are just tender. Turn off the heat and let the rings stand in the pan for a moment.

Makes 12 onion rings.

Variations: Use ½ pork and ½ beef. Note that the pork is more tender when cooked.
Substitute bread crumbs for the bean curd; they have the same softening effect.

SOGOGI HOBAK NAMUL
ZUCCHINI WITH BEEF

1 pound zucchini
2 teaspoons salt
2 cloves garlic
1 tablespoon sesame oil

¼ pound ground beef
dash black pepper
1 tablespoon soy sauce

1. Slice the zucchini in half lengthwise, then cut each half into pieces ¼ inch thick. Mix the pieces with salt and let stand for 1 hour. Squeeze out as much water as possible.

2. Crush the garlic. Heat the sesame oil in a frying pan and brown the beef, separating the pieces. Add the garlic and season with pepper. Add the zucchini and cook for no longer than 5 minutes over a high flame. Remove from the heat and stir in the soy sauce.

Makes 2 to 4 servings.

KOCHU CHUNYUA
STUFFED GREEN PEPPER QUARTERS

Stuffed green pepper quarters are an excellent side dish or appetizer.

2 to 3 green peppers	½ teaspoon salt
½ teaspoon salt	½ teaspoon sesame seeds
1 scallion	½ teaspoon sesame oil
2 cloves garlic	pinch black pepper
¼ pound ground beef	3 tablespoons flour
2-inch slice of bean curd	2 eggs
(2 ounces)	⅓ cup sesame oil

1. Quarter the peppers and remove all the seeds. Sprinkle with salt.

2. Mince the scallion and crush the garlic. Combine these ingredients with the beef, bean curd, salt, sesame seeds, sesame oil and pepper in a bowl. Mix well.

3. Flour the inside of the pepper quarters. Pat the meat mixture into the center depression. Dip the quarters into the flour. Beat the eggs slightly. Dip the quarters into the eggs.

4. Heat the oil in a skillet. Sauté the peppers meat-side down until browned, then turn them over. Reduce the heat and cook for about 5 minutes or until peppers are just tender. Turn off the heat and let the quarters stand in the pan for a moment.

Makes 8 to 12 green pepper quarters, depending on the size of the peppers.

Variations: Substitute bread crumbs for the bean curd.

Use ½ pound beef and ½ pound pork or all pork.

OI BOKUM
CUCUMBER WITH PORK

3 cucumbers	¼ pound ground pork
1 tablespoon salt	1 tablespoon sesame oil
2 scallions	dash pepper
2 cloves garlic	2 tablespoons soy sauce
¼ pound ground beef	1 teaspoon sesame seeds

1. Slice the cucumbers in circles (not too fine). Sprinkle with salt and mix well. Let the slices stand for 30 minutes, then place them in a damp cloth and squeeze out as much water as possible.

2. Cut the scallions into ¼-inch lengths, using the green stalks. Crush the garlic. Combine the beef, pork, garlic and scallions in a bowl.

3. Heat the sesame oil in a skillet and brown the meat well, crushing out all the lumps. Season with pepper and soy sauce. Add the cucumber and stir-fry for 2 minutes. Garnish with sesame seeds.

Makes 4 servings.

PUCHOU BOKUM
PORK WITH CHINESE CHIVES

The taste of cooked Chinese chives is faintly reminiscent
of spinach, but their texture is firmer and their flavor
more nutlike. This dish may be served hot, warm or cold.

½ pound lean pork
½ pound Chinese chives
2 hot peppers (red, if
   possible, and 3 inches
   long)

2 tablespoons sesame oil
¼ cup soy sauce
1 heaping tablespoon
   sesame seeds

1. Shred the pork into match-shaped pieces 2 inches
long. Cut the meat across the grain. Clean the chives, then
cut them into 2-inch lengths. Seed the peppers by
cutting down one side. Open them flat and shred
across the grain.

2. Heat the sesame oil in a heavy skillet. Brown the pork
strips quickly. Add the Chinese chives and turn the
strips over several times so that the oil coats all sides. Add
the peppers. When the chives begin to wilt, add the soy
sauce and remove immediately from the heat.

3. Mix well with the sesame seeds.

Makes 2 to 4 servings.

CHEYUK KAJI CHIM
PORK-STUFFED EGGPLANT

Serve pork-stuffed eggplant as an appetizer or a side dish.

1 medium eggplant, preferably long and thin	½ teaspoon salt
	½ teaspoon sesame seeds
¼ teaspoon salt	½ teaspoon sesame oil
1 scallion	pinch black pepper
2 cloves garlic	3 tablespoons flour
¼ pound ground pork	2 eggs
2-inch slice of bean curd (2 ounces)	⅓ cup sesame oil

1. Cut the eggplant into ½-inch round slices. Cut out the center of the rings, leaving a hole the size of a nickel. Sprinkle the rings with salt.

2. Mince the scallion and crush the garlic. Combine these ingredients with the pork, bean curd, salt, sesame seeds, sesame oil and pepper in a bowl. Mix well.

3. Dip the eggplant rings into the flour. Pat the meat mixture into the center cavity and on top of the slices. Dip the rings into the flour. Beat the eggs slightly in a bowl. Dip the rings into the eggs.

4. Heat the oil in a skillet. Sauté the rings meat-side down until browned, then turn them over. Reduce the heat and cook for about 5 minutes or until the eggplant is just tender. Turn off the heat and let the rings stand in the hot pan for a moment.

Makes 12 rings.

Variations: Substitute bread crumbs for the bean curd. Use ½ pound beef and ½ pound pork.

CHAEYUK KO CHU CHAE
GREEN PEPPERS WITH PORK

¼ pound lean pork
3 bell peppers
1 large clove garlic
2 scallions
1 tablespoon sesame oil

dash black pepper
2 tablespoons soy sauce
1 tablespoon sesame
　seeds

1. Shred the pork into match-shaped pieces. Quarter the peppers, then slice them thin across the grain. Mince the garlic. Cut the scallions into 2-inch pieces.

2. Heat ½ tablespoon sesame oil in a pan and add the pork. Stir-fry until brown. Add the garlic, scallions and black pepper. Stir for a moment. Add the remaining oil and green peppers. Cook for no longer than 5 minutes or until just tender. Add soy sauce 1 minute before removing from pan.

3. Arrange on a serving dish and garnish with the sesame seeds. Serve immediately.

Makes 2 to 4 servings.

HOBAK NAMUL
ZUCCHINI WITH CHICKEN

1 pound zucchini	1 tablespoon sesame oil
2 teaspoons salt	dash black pepper
¼ pound chicken breast	1 tablespoon soy sauce
2 cloves garlic	

1. Slice the zucchini into circles ⅛ inch thick, then shred the rounds into thin finger-shaped pieces. Mix well with salt and let them stand for 1 hour. Squeeze out as much water as possible.

2. Shred the chicken into finger-shaped pieces. Crush the garlic.

3. Heat the sesame oil in a skillet. Brown the chicken and season with garlic and pepper. Add the zucchini and cook for 5 minutes maximum over a high flame. Serve as a salad at room temperature.

Makes 2 to 4 servings.

DAK HOBAK CHUNYUA
CHICKEN-STUFFED ZUCCHINI

Chicken-stuffed zucchini makes an attractive side dish
or a delicious appetizer.

2 zucchini
¼ teaspoon salt
¼ pound ground chicken
1 scallion
2 cloves garlic
2-inch slice of bean curd
   (2 ounces)

½ teaspoon salt
½ teaspoon sesame seeds
½ teaspoon sesame oil
pinch black pepper
3 tablespoons flour
2 eggs
⅓ cup sesame oil

1. Slice the zucchini into ½-inch round slices. Cut out
the center of the slices, leaving a hole the size of a nickel.
(The size of the zucchini will determine the size of the
center cavity.) Sprinkle the slices with salt.

2. Mince the scallion and crush the garlic. Combine these
ingredients with the chicken, bean curd, salt, sesame
seeds, sesame oil and pepper in a bowl. Mix well.

3. Dip the zucchini slices into the flour. Pat the chicken
mixture into the center cavity and on top of the zucchini.
Dip the slices into the flour. Beat the eggs slightly.
Dip the slices into the eggs.

4. Heat the oil in a skillet. Sauté the zucchini slices meat-side down until browned, then turn them over. Reduce the heat and cook for about 4 to 5 minutes or until the zucchini are just tender. Turn off the heat and let the slices stand in the pan for a moment.

Makes 12 to 16 slices.

DAK NAENGCHAE
COLD VEGETABLES WITH CHICKEN

Easy to prepare, this salad recipe is suggested as a good "Sunday night" supper.

1 2½-pound chicken
water to cover
2 dried black mushrooms
1 carrot
1 leaf Chinese cabbage
1 small cucumber
2 scallions
2 large fresh mushrooms
1 teaspoon salt
1½ tablespoons sugar
1 teaspoon soy sauce

2 cloves garlic, crushed
1 teaspoon white vinegar
1 teaspoon pine nuts
1½ tablespoons sesame
   seeds
⅓ cup chicken broth
1 tablespoon dried
   mustard
1 tablespoon boiling
   water

1. Cover the chicken with water and bring to a boil. Skim off the froth and allow to simmer for 1 hour or until done.

2. Soak the dried black mushrooms in boiling water for 30 minutes, then shred them into thin finger-shaped pieces. Slice the carrot into thin strips 1½ inches long. Cut the Chinese cabbage into 1½-inch lengths, then shred. Cut the cucumber in half. With a spoon remove the seeds, leaving only the solid outer part. Cut the outer part into 1½-inch lengths, then shred. Cut the scallions into 1½-inch lengths, then shred. Slice the fresh mushrooms.

3. Combine all the vegetables in a bowl and sprinkle with salt. Mix well. Let the vegetables stand for 15 minutes, then rinse very quickly under cold water and squeeze out as much water as possible.

4. Add the sugar, soy sauce, crushed garlic, vinegar, pine nuts, sesame seeds and chicken broth to the vegetables. Bone the chicken and cut it into 2-inch serving-size pieces. Make a paste of dried mustard and 1 tablespoon boiling water. Add the mustard and mix well.

Makes 4 servings.

CHAP CHAE
MIXED VEGETABLES I

¼ pound beef strips (flank steak, chuck steak or sirloin)
1 cup transparent noodles, soaked
2 Chinese mushrooms
1 carrot
1 small zucchini
1 onion
3 scallions
½ red bell pepper
4 large button mushrooms
3 tablespoons sesame oil
salt
white or red pepper to taste
egg decoration

1. Slice about 10 strips from the flank steak. Cut these strips into smaller strips of finger-length size.

2. Soak the noodles in hot water to cover for 15 minutes, then drain. Soak the Chinese mushrooms in water for 30 minutes before slicing.

3. Cut the carrot and zucchini into 3 pieces. Slice each piece lengthwise as thin as possible, then shred into fine strips. Slice the onion thin. Cut the scallions, bell pepper and both kinds of mushrooms into thin lengths 2 inches long.

4. Heat the oil in a large frying pan and sauté the beef strips until they are slightly browned. Add the combined vegetables and cook over a high flame, stirring constantly for 2 minutes. Add the transparent noodles, stir, add salt and red pepper to taste. Allow to simmer for 4 minutes longer.

5. Place the vegetables on a large serving dish and garnish with the egg decoration.

Makes 4 to 6 servings.

CHAP CHAE
MIXED VEGETABLES II

Use any combination of 3 or more vegetables which contrast in color, beef, one type of mushroom and transparent noodles.

½ pound flank steak
carrot
onion
scallion
red bell pepper
green bell pepper
zucchini
Chinese mushrooms
button mushrooms
bamboo shoots

Chinese cabbage
1 cup transparent
    noodles, soaked
cloud-ear mushrooms
1 clove garlic
1 teaspoon soy sauce
2 tablespoons sesame oil
pinch salt
pinch pepper

1. Slice the beef thin on the bias. Cut again lengthwise into thin strips about 1½ inches long. Cut the vegetables lengthwise into fine strips about 2½ inches long. Mince the garlic. Soak the noodles and mushrooms in water for 30 minutes or until soft.

2. Heat the oil and sauté the beef until browned. Add the vegetables and garlic. Cook over a high flame for 4 minutes, stirring as necessary. Add the soaked noodles, soy sauce, salt and pepper. Cook for an additional minute to blend the flavors.

Makes 4 servings.

KEJA

MUSTARD SAUCE FOR KUJOL PAN
AND WON DU CHE

½ cup dried mustard   ¼ teaspoon salt
2 tablespoons sugar   1 tablespoon soy sauce

Combine all ingredients in a bowl and serve with the
crêpes.

KUJOL PAN
NINE-COURSE HORS D'OEUVRE TRAY

Kujol Pan is one of the most time-consuming and
elaborate dishes to be found in Korean cookery.
Generally served on special occasions, it is as visually
attractive as it is savory. Special dishes similar to French
hors-d'oeuvres trays are manufactured to serve this
festive recipe.

Basic

1½ medium cucumbers
½ teaspoon salt
dash pepper
1 teaspoon sesame oil

¼ pound lean pork
⅛ teaspoon salt
1 teaspoon sesame oil

¼ pound beef (flank
    steak)
⅛ teaspoon salt
1 teaspoon sesame oil

¼ pound abalone
    (canned)

pinch salt
1 teaspoon sesame oil

1 cup Chinese cabbage
    (after cutting)
⅛ teaspoon salt
1 teaspoon sesame oil

1 cup mushrooms
⅛ teaspoon salt
1 teaspoon sesame oil

3 eggs
¼ teaspoon salt
1 teaspoon sesame oil

1 pear
1 peach

Crêpes

7 tablespoons flour
1 tablespoon potato
  starch
2 teaspoons sugar

¼ teaspoon salt
1 egg
¾ cup beef stock
sesame oil

Basic:

1. Slit the cucumbers down the center. Remove the seeds
with a spoon. Slice each half into thin strips about 2
inches long. Sprinkle with salt and mix well. Let the strips
stand for 30 minutes while the other ingredients are
being prepared, then squeeze out as much water
as possible.

2. Slice the pork thin on the bias, then again into thin
strips 1½ inches long. Slice the beef in the same fashion.
Cut the abalone and Chinese cabbage into thin strips.
Keep each ingredient separate. Quarter the mushrooms.

3. Beat the eggs together with the salt. Use a brush or a
paper towel to oil a large skillet. Pour off any excess oil.
When the skillet is very hot, pour in some of the eggs.
Cook them until they are just firm. Turn them over and
cook on the other side for a moment; do not brown them.
The eggs should be spread as thin as possible. Repeat
this process until all the eggs have been used.
Cut the eggs into thin strips.

4. Sauté the cucumbers in the sesame oil. Arrange a small pile of cucumbers on a serving platter. Sauté separately the beef, pork, abalone, Chinese cabbage and mushrooms, adding the required seasonings while cooking. Do not overcook the vegetables; they should be tender. Arrange each ingredient separately in small mounds on a serving platter.

Crêpes
5. Combine the flour, starch, sugar, salt and egg in a bowl. While stirring ingredients well, slowly add the stock. Oil the bottom of a large frying pan with a brush or paper towel dipped in sesame oil. Pour off any excess oil. Pour in just enough crêpe mixture to cover the bottom of the pan. Cook the mixture for a minute or until the crêpe can be picked up and turned over. (Fingers are suggested for this operation.) Cook on the other side until firm. Do not brown the crepe. The ingredients should make 3 large crêpes; to make the others, oil the pan, and then repeat.

6. Place the 3 large crêpes one on top of the other. Using a water glass, cut out 4 circles. There should now be 12 small crêpes. Place these crêpes in the center of a serving platter. Use some of the mustard sauce, *keja,* on the crêpes.

7. Slice the pear and peach thin, then slice them again into thin strips. They must be sliced immediately before serving, or they will turn brown when exposed to the air.

Makes 4 to 8 servings with other dishes.

Variations: Substitute shrimp for abalone.

Use cloud-ear mushrooms or dried Chinese mushrooms and soak them before sautéing.

A variety of vegetables may be used: zucchini, carrots, bean sprouts. But no substitutions must be made for pork, egg or beef.

The egg whites may also be separated from the yolks before preparing the egg decoration. This separation provides an attractive color contrast.

WON DU CHAE
THE WATCHMAN'S SALAD

The watchman in the rice fields finds the long day a lonely vigil, so a friend may keep him company. They play Korean chess or cards and sometimes have a delightful picnic of Won Du Che.

Won Du Che, now an elaborate party dish, owes its particular flavor to sea cucumber. Its preparation will provide a challenge, even to the master cook.

Basic

1 cup sea cucumber
½ cup canned bamboo
   shoots, sliced
½ cup cloud-ear
   mushrooms, soaked
5 button mushrooms
2 scallions
½ pound flank steak
½ carrot
½ pound or 3 cups
   Chinese cabbage

1 teaspoon ginger
2 cloves garlic
5 shrimp
2 tablespoons sesame oil
⅓ cup soy sauce
⅓ cup beef stock
dash black pepper
1 teaspoon potato starch
2 tablespoons stock
1 cup water

Crêpes

1 egg
¼ teaspoon salt
4 tablespoons potato
   starch
1 tablespoon flour

⅓ cup stock
sesame oil
mustard sauce
egg decoration (optional)

1. Soak the sea cucumber in water for 1 week. If pressed for time, place it in a pot with 10 cups hot water. Bring to a boil and simmer for 3 to 3½ hours. Using a knife, scrape off the cucumber's prickles. They peel off easily under cold water. Open the sea cucumber and clean out the inside. There is a white membrane-like skin which is not good to eat.

2. Slice the bamboo shoots thin. Soak the cloud-ear mushrooms in warm water. Slice the button mushrooms. Cut the scallions into 1-inch lengths. Slice the beef thin on the bias into 1-inch lengths. Slice the carrot on the bias. Cut the Chinese cabbage into 1-inch squares. Slice the ginger into thin slivers. Slice the garlic into thin slivers. Shell and de-vein the shrimp. Flatten the shrimp by cutting to, but not through the outer edge down the center. The tail will hold the body together.

3. Crêpes: Break I egg into a bowl then add salt, potato starch and flour. Mix these ingredients well, then slowly add the stock. Oil the bottom of a large skillet with a paper towel dipped in sesame oil. Pour just enough of the crêpe mixture into the pan to cover the bottom. Cook this mixture for a minute. Turn the mixture over. (Fingers are suggested for this operation.) Cook for a minute. Oil the pan again and cook the remaining crêpe

mixture. These ingredients will make 2 large crêpes.
Cut the crêpes into wedges as for a pie. Spread some of
the mustard sauce, *keja,* (see page 215) over the wedges.

4. Heat 2 tablespoons sesame oil in a skillet and sauté the
sea cucumber, bamboo shoots, mushrooms, scallions,
steak, carrot, cabbage, ginger and garlic over a high flame.
After 3 to 4 minutes, when the vegetables are just
tender, add the soy sauce, stock and pepper. Combine the
potato starch with 2 tablespoons stock and stir into the
vegetables in order to thicken the sauce.

5. Bring the shrimp to a boil in 1 cup water. (They are
done as soon as they boil.) Add 1 tablespoon
mustard sauce.

6. Place the vegetables on a serving platter. Arrange the
crêpe wedges around the edge of the platter. Place
the shrimp on top of the vegetables.

Makes 4 to 6 servings.

Variation: Garnish with the egg decoration.

WON DU SAM
THE WATCHTOWER PICNIC

Perched among the rice fields are tiny watchtowers, low platforms with a grass roof on which the watchman sits. He is a human scarecrow whose job it is to keep the crows away from the grains. The following recipe is what his wife may bring him for lunch.

This dish, now a good recipe to serve guests, is a combination of meat and vegetables wrapped in small, thin, very soft crêpes.

Basic

½ cup cloud-ear mushrooms, soaked
1 cup Chinese cabbage, sliced
¼ pound flank steak
1 cup cucumber, sliced
5 scallions

5 button mushrooms
2 cloves garlic
1 tablespoon sesame oil
½ teaspoon salt
dash pepper
1 tablespoon sesame seeds

Crêpes

3 tablespoons potato starch
1 egg
¼ teaspoon salt

1 teaspoon sugar
⅓ cup beef stock
sesame oil

1. Soak the cloud-ear mushrooms in water. Slice the cabbage into thin finger-shaped pieces 2 inches long.

Slice the steak on the bias, then into thin finger-shaped pieces 2 inches long. Slice the cucumber in the same manner. Slice the scallions into 2-inch lengths, then into slivers. Slice the button mushrooms and the garlic into slivers. Chop the cloud-ear mushrooms coarsely.

2. Crêpes: Combine the starch, egg, salt and sugar in a bowl. Stir in the stock slowly. Oil the bottom of a large skillet with a paper towel dipped in sesame oil. The skillet should be very hot before the crêpe mixture is added. Pour in enough mixture to cover the bottom of the pan. When the mixture is firm but not browned, turn it over. (Fingers are suggested for this operation.) Cook until firm. Oil the pan, then make another crêpe in the same manner. Using a water glass, cut out 4 circles from each crêpe.

3. Heat 1 tablespoon sesame oil in a skillet. Brown the meat and garlic quickly. Add the cabbage, cucumber, scallions, button and cloud-ear mushrooms. Cook until the vegetables are tender. Add the salt and pepper. Sprinkle with the sesame seeds.

4. Arrange the vegetables on a large platter in 8 small mounds. Place one crêpe on top of each mound. Serve immediately.

Makes 4 to 6 servings.

HAPPINESS POT SAUCE

⅓ cup kochu chang
  (see page 263)
⅓ cup vinegar
¼ cup sugar

1 tablespoon sesame oil
1 tablespoon roasted
  sesame seeds

Combine all the ingredients in a bowl and mix well. Place
a small amount in a saucer, one per person, so that
each may dip his food into the sauce easily.

SOGOGI DECHIM WHE
HAPPINESS POT WITH BEEF

Happiness pot with beef is an excellent company dish. All the ingredients can be prepared in advance and cooked in a chafing dish at the table. The ingredients must be sliced so fine that there is no need to boil them. They are cooked when warm.

3 pounds sirloin steak
½ pound Chinese
   cabbage leaves (about 4
   large leaves)
10 scallions
10 mushrooms
½ pound onions
½ pound yellow soybean
   sprouts
2 large hot peppers (about
   3 inches long)

5 cloves garlic
1 inch fresh ginger
1 cake bean curd
1 ounce transparent
   noodles
2 tablespoons to ½ cup
   kochu chang (see
   page 263)
2 cups beef stock

1. Slice the steak thin into pieces 3 inches long and 1 inch wide. Slice the cabbage leaves across the grain into 2-inch lengths. Cut the scallions into 2-inch lengths. Slice the mushrooms. Cut the onions in half, then cut each half into 3 or 4 fairly thick slices across the grain. Remove the root ends from the yellow bean sprouts, wash and drain.

2. Seed the hot peppers by making a cut down the center, then shred across the grain. Slice the garlic thin. Cut the ginger into slivers. Halve the bean cake, then cut each half into about 5 pieces. Drop the thread noodles into boiling water. Boil for 2 minutes, then drain.

3. Mix the kochu chang into the beef stock. Use this mixture as a base in the chafing dish. A moment's immersion in the simmering broth should be sufficient time to cook the meat. It is important not to overcook the meat. This beef may be eaten rare. Serve with Happiness Pot Sauce.

Makes 6 servings.

Variations: Use regular bean sprouts and 1 sliced lotus root. Add 1 carrot cut into 2-inch lengths, thinly sliced. Use American cabbage cut into 2-inch squares.

BOK NAM BI
HAPPINESS POT WITH SHELL FISH

In spite of its length, this recipe is not difficult, and is convenient when you are expecting guests, since the ingredients can be gathered in advance, and the cooking is done at the table. You will need a chafing dish on the table, or an electric frying pan will do, although it lacks the proper aesthetic appeal. The hostess should cook the various shell fish herself and serve each of the guests in turn. Later on when the vegetables are added, the guests may help themselves from the communal pot.

Because the cooking of the shell fish and the vegetables allows the hostess to display her culinary art and gracefulness at the table, the Happiness Pot is a favorite in Kiesseng houses.

¼ pound canned abalone
½ pound squid
5 jumbo shrimp
10 clams
10 oysters
½ pound Chinese cabbage leaves (about 4 large ones)
10 scallions
10 mushrooms
½ pound onions
½ pound yellow soybean sprouts
2 large hot peppers (one red, one green about 3 inches long)
5 cloves garlic
1 inch fresh ginger
1 cake bean curd
1 ounce thread noodles
2 cups beef stock
½ cup kochu chang (see page 263)

1. Prepare a very large platter on which all the raw ingredients may be attractively arranged.

2. Slice abalone very thinly. Clean squid. (See page 166) Cut in half lengthwise, then slice across the grain into 2 inch widths. Shell (or have fish dealer shell) clams and oysters, but do not cut them. Shell shrimps, cut in half lengthwise, leaving the tail attached. De-vein shrimp. Slice cabbage leaves across the grain into 2 inch lengths. Cut scallions into 2 inch lengths. Slice mushrooms. Cut onions in half then into 3 or 4 fairly thick slices across the grain. Remove root ends from yellow soybeans, wash, drain. Seed the hot peppers by making one cut down the center, then shred across the grain. Slice garlic thin. Cut ginger into slivers. Halve the bean cake then cut into about 5 pieces. Place thread noodles in boiling water for 2 minutes then drain.

3. Mix kochu chang into the beef stock. Use this as the base in the chafing dish on the table. The platter of seafood and vegetables should be placed beside the hostess, with the chafing dish in front of her so that she may conveniently cook and serve the other guests. It is important that the seafood not be overcooked. Usually a moment's immersion in the simmering broth is enough to cook the fish. Remember that most of these fish could

be eaten raw, and so the longer they boil, the tougher they will become.

Makes 6 servings. Serve with Happiness Pot Sauce.

Variations: Use a conch instead of abalone. Prepare the conch as follows:

The conch should weigh about ½ pound with its shell. Bring a pot of water to a boil, add the conch, bring to a second boil and boil for a good minute or two. Drain, remove the conch from its shell, and wash under cold running water, removing its innards. Slice thin. Do not be frightened by its looks, you may eat all of it.

YUNGUN CHANGUA
LOTUS ROOTS

Lotus roots make a superb lunch, snack or picnic treat.

1 pound lotus roots
3 cups water
¼ cup vinegar
6½ teaspoons soy sauce
½ cup sugar

¼ cup sherry
1 tablespoon unground
    roasted sesame seeds
    (optional)

1. Slice the lotus roots thin, into circles. Bring the water
and vinegar to a boil in a medium-sized saucepan.
(Vinegar preserves the lotus roots' fresh color.) Add the
lotus root circles. Bring to a second boil and continue
boiling vigorously for 3 minutes. Remove the saucepan
from the heat. Drain, but do not rinse the circles.

2. Place the soy sauce, sugar and sherry in a heavy skillet.
Bring to a boil and add the lotus circles. Cook, covered,
for 15 minutes. Stir often, turning the circles so that
both sides are well seasoned. Do not let the sugar burn or
stick to the bottom of the pan. If the sauce has evaporated
before the 15 minutes have elapsed, remove from heat.

3. Garnish with sesame seeds. This dish may be served
immediately or covered and refrigerated. Cooked
lotus roots may be stored for 2 weeks.

Makes 3 to 6 servings.

KIMCHI AND SALADS

GUT CHURI KIMCHI
INSTANT KIMCHI

Kimchi, for better or worse, finds its way to the table
daily, like bread in the West. It should be made in
the home with loving care, and the following recipes are
some simple and not-so-simple ways of making various
types of kimchi. If this activity seems just too much for
you, you can purchase jars of ready-made Kimchi
in most Japanese food stores.

1 Chinese cabbage
2 cloves garlic
1 teaspoon hot pepper
1 tablespoon soy sauce

1 teaspoon vinegar
1 tablespoon salt
1 tablespoon sugar

1. Chop the cabbage into pieces about 1½ inches long
by 1½ inches wide. Three cups of chopped cabbage
are needed.

2. Crush the garlic and blend with the hot pepper, soy
sauce and vinegar. Add the cabbage and mix well. Add
the salt and sugar, mix and cover until ready to serve.

Makes 4 servings.

MU SANGCHAE
TURNIP SALAD

Chinese turnip is used in many kimchi-type dishes and fortunately does not require the waiting period that kimchi does. If an authentic Korean dinner is desired and there is no kimchi readily available or there is not sufficient time to prepare it, substitute turnip salad.

¾ pound Chinese turnip
3 scallions
1 inch fresh ginger root or ½ teaspoon powdered ginger
3 cloves garlic
1 teaspoon salt

2 teaspoons white vinegar
2 teaspoons sugar
1 teaspoon sesame oil
1 teaspoon sesame seeds
½ to 2½ teaspoons hot cayenne pepper

1. Slice the turnip into circles ⅛ inch thick, then slice again crosswise into thin finger-shaped pieces. Slice the scallions into finger-shaped pieces 2 inches long. Cut 1 clove garlic and the ginger in the same fashion, but as fine as possible. Crush the other 2 cloves garlic.

2. Place these ingredients in a bowl and mix well with the salt, white vinegar, sugar, sesame oil and sesame seeds. Add ½ teaspoon hot pepper; taste and add more until the desired hot flavor has been reached.

Makes 2 to 4 servings.

DONG CHIMI
TURNIP-WATER KIMCHI

Turnip-water kimchi has a light refreshing taste. One of the easiest kimchi recipes to prepare, it is a good starting point for a beginning kimchi enthusiast.

1 pound Chinese turnip	2 cloves garlic
1 scallion	1 tablespoon salt
1 tablespoon fresh ginger	

2 cups water	½ teaspoon sugar
1 tablespoon salt	

1. Slice the turnip into finger-shaped pieces, 1½ inches long and ½ inch wide. Cut the scallion into 1½-inch lengths, then slice fine lengthwise. Repeat the same process for the ginger and garlic. Place these ingredients in a bowl, sprinkle with salt, mix well and leave, covered, overnight.

2. Mix 2 cups water with the salt and sugar in a separate bowl. Let this mixture stand overnight, then pour it over the kimchi. Keep at room temperature for 24 hours. Transfer to jars and refrigerate. It will keep for at least 1 week.

MAK KIMCHI I
CASUAL KIMCHI

As the name implies, this recipe is not for a grandiose production of kimchi. Casual kimchi can be made in 10 minutes and will be ready to eat after a two-day waiting period.

4 pounds Chinese
   cabbage (the long,
   straight leafed variety)
¼ pound Chinese turnip
2 cans flat anchovies
kat (optional)
4 to 5 cloves garlic

3 scallions
¼ cup salt
4 tablespoons hot pepper
   flakes
2 tablespoons cayenne
   pepper

1. Remove the large outside leaves of the cabbage. Cut them in half lengthwise, then cut across the grain into 2-inch lengths. Cut all the inside leaves into 2-inch lengths at the same time. Place the cabbage in a very large pot.

2. Quarter the turnip, then slice across the grain holding the 4 quarters together for more speed and convenience in slicing.

3. Pour the oil from the anchovies over the cabbage and turnip. Slice the anchovies across the grain and slice the kat into 2-inch lengths. Crush the garlic. Cut the scallions into 2-inch lengths, then slice thin lengthwise. Add these ingredients to the pot. Season with salt, pepper flakes and cayenne pepper, and mix thoroughly. Cover the pot and let the mixture stand at room temperature for 2 days. Casual kimchi will keep at least 10 days. Refrigerate in a jar.

MAK KIMCHI II
QUICK KIMCHI

The making of kimchi poses a problem for the busy
housewife. The turnips and cabbages need to be pickled
days before they are to be eaten, yet a Korean meal is not
authentic without kimchi. This version, however, will
provide a small quantity and is quick to prepare.

1½ pounds Chinese turnip
1½ pounds Chinese cabbage
1 cup water
¼ cup salt
4 large scallions

4 large cloves garlic or 6 small cloves
2 tablespoons chopped fresh ginger
7 teaspoons cayenne pepper

1. Wash the leaves of a Chinese cabbage and cut them
into 2-inch lengths (the leafy end may be left longer;
it will shrivel the most). Peel the Chinese turnip, halve it
lengthwise down the center and then slice
thin across the grain.

2. Combine the salt and water. Place the vegetables in a
large pot. Pour the salted water over the surface of
the vegetables and cover the pot. Leave overnight.

3. The next day, mince the scallions, garlic and ginger. Drain the vegetables, which should be wilted, and reserve the salty water. Season with the cayenne, scallion, garlic and ginger. Mix the vegetables by hand, using rubber gloves if available. Pack this mixture tightly into jars. Pour the salted water over the mixture so that the liquid comes to within ½ inch of the top of the jar.

4. Keep at room temperature for 2 or 3 days, then refrigerate.

Makes about 2 jars of kimchi which should be enough for a large dinner party.

NABAK KIMCHI
WATER KIMCHI

1 2-pound Chinese
   cabbage (the curly-
   leafed variety)
1 pound Chinese turnip
2 scallions
2 tablespoons fresh ginger

3 large cloves garlic
1 teaspoon cayenne
   pepper
1 teaspoon string pepper
   (optional)
2 tablespoons salt

4 cups water
2 tablespoons salt

½ teaspoon sugar

1. Remove the outer leaves of the cabbage. Cut them in half or in thirds, then slice across the grain into 1-inch wide pieces. The small inner leaves may be sliced into squares. Cut the turnip into 1-inch squares about ¼ inch thick. Slice the scallions into 1½-inch lengths, then slice again lengthwise, into fine finger-shaped pieces. Repeat this process for the ginger and garlic. Add the cayenne pepper. While mixing well, sprinkle slowly with salt. Let the mixture stand overnight, covered.

2. Mix the water, salt and sugar in a bowl. Pour this solution over the cabbage and turnip mixture. Mix, cover and let it stand at room temperature for 25 hours. Place in jars and refrigerate.

SOBAEGI KIMCHI
STUFFED KIMCHI

Stuffed kimchi is a classic dish and if properly made may be considered an artistic achievement. It is found in most Korean households and is a fitting accompaniment to every Korean meal.

4 pounds Chinese cabbage (the short curly-leafed variety)
1 cup salt
12 cups water
1 pound Chinese turnip
6 scallions
6 cloves garlic
6 oysters

1 inch fresh ginger or ¼ teaspoon ginger powder
1 tablespoon salted baby shrimp
1 tablespoon salt
5 teaspoons hot cayenne pepper
5 cups beef stock
1 tablespoon salt

1. Slice the cabbage into quarters from top to bottom and place in a pot. Mix the salt and water, then pour over the cabbage quarters and allow to stand for 24 hours.

2. Shred the turnip into paper-thin finger-shaped pieces 2½ inches long. Slice the scallions into 2½-inch lengths, then shred. Crush the garlic. Slice the oysters.

3. In a bowl mix together the turnip, scallions, garlic, oysters, ginger, baby shrimp, salt and red pepper. Drain the cabbage and rinse slightly under cold water if it tastes very salty. Lift up each leaf and place some mixture between each one. The last leaf should be wrapped around the bottom of the quarter to hold the rest of the mixture in place. Place the quarters with the outside leaf facing down in a large pot. As the liquid drains from the inside, the outside pieces will be flavored.

4. Pour the beef stock mixed with salt over the cabbage. Push the cabbage down very firmly. Leave in a covered pot for 3 days.

5. Serve the stuffed kimchi sliced across the grain into 1½-inch pieces. It will keep 2 or more weeks in the refrigerator.

Makes 8 to 10 servings.

OI SOBAEGI KIMCHI
CUCUMBER KIMCHI

The varicolored turnip mixture used as stuffing for this recipe makes cucumber kimchi a visually appealing addition to any meal. Select small thin cucumbers like those used in making dill pickles.

1 large cucumber or 5
    small cucumbers
2 tablespoons salt
2 cups water
1 pound Chinese turnip
¼ carrot
2 cloves garlic
2 scallions
3 hot red peppers

¼ teaspoon powdered
    ginger or 1 teaspoon
    fresh ginger
1 teaspoon salt
1 teaspoon sugar
¾ teaspoon cayenne
    pepper
1 cup chicken stock or
    bouillon cube

1. Make 3 deep slashes at equal intervals lengthwise down the cucumbers. Do not cut the ends; the cucumbers must remain whole.

2. Dissolve 2 tablespoons salt in 2 cups water and soak the cucumbers in this solution for 2 hours. The cucumbers will then be so pliable that they can be stuffed without cracking open.

3. Slice the turnip into circles, then again into thread-like, finger-shaped pieces. Slice the carrot into thin finger-shaped pieces. Crush the garlic. Slice the scallions into 1½-inch lengths, then into fine finger-shaped pieces. Remove the seeds from the red peppers and mince. Mince the ginger. Mix the turnip and all seasonings well.

4. Squeeze as much water as possible from the cucumbers. Stuff the turnip mixture into each of the 3 slots as tightly as possible. Place in a jar along with any stuffing that may remain. Let stand for 3 hours, then pour 1 cup chicken stock into the jar. Let stand at room temperature for 24 hours, then refrigerate.

KAKTUGUI
TURNIP SQUARES

4 pounds Chinese turnip	¼ cup baby salted shrimp
4 scallions	¼ cup hot cayenne
6 cloves garlic	pepper
30 oysters	1 tablespoon sugar

1. Quarter the turnip, then slice into ¾-inch thicknesses, but do not peel. Cut the scallions into 2-inch lengths, then shred as thin as possible. Crush the garlic. Slice the oysters thin.

2. Mix together all these ingredients with the shrimp, pepper and sugar. Use rubber gloves or toss as for a salad. Let the ingredients stand, covered, for 3 hours or overnight. Refrigerate in jars.

Variations: The turnip may be cut into squares, ¾ inch by 1¼ inches. For a long-lasting kimchi, cut the turnip into pieces ¼ inch by 1¼ inches by 1¼ inches.

PUCHOU CHANG-A-CHI
CHINESE CHIVES WITH SALTED SHRIMP

Chinese chives with salted shrimp is a very unusual and strong-tasting salad which must be prepared 2 or 3 days before it is served.

¼ pound Chinese chives
1 heaping tablespoon
   baby salted shrimp
1 tablespoon soy sauce
1 tablespoon sesame oil

2 cloves chopped garlic
1 tablespoon cayenne
   pepper
1 tablespoon sugar

1. Remove the faded leaves and brown skin from the stems of the chives. Wash the chives in cold water, rubbing the ends together. Cut them into 2-inch lengths.

2. Combine the shrimp, soy sauce, sesame oil, chopped garlic, cayenne pepper and sugar in a bowl. Add the Chinese chives and mix well.

3. Pack the chive mixture tightly into a jar. Twenty-four hours later, invert the jar. The juices will then penetrate the upper half of the mixture. Keep at room temperature for 2 days. The mixture may then be eaten or refrigerated.

Makes 4 servings.

RICE

BAB
STEAMED RICE

Generally speaking, if Americans are to be served, use
½ cup uncooked rice for each person. Double the
amount if cooking for Koreans, especially Korean men.

2 cups rice   2 cups water

1. Pour the rice into a cooking pot. Fill the pot nearly to
the brim with cold water, then pour the water out. The
rice will remain at the bottom of the pot. Repeat this
process 4 or 5 times, or until the water seems quite clear.
Rinsing the rice in this manner eliminates
any excess starch.

2. Cover the rice with 2 cups water and let it stand for
30 minutes. Bring to a boil, reduce the heat and steam for
20 minutes or until dry.

Makes 4 servings.

BAM BAB
RICE WITH CHESTNUTS

In the autumn when fresh chestnuts are available, they may be added to rice to dress it up.

2 cups rice   2 cups shelled chestnuts
1¾ cups water

1. Wash the rice. Cover the rice with water and let stand for 30 minutes.

2. Shell the chestnuts and add them to the rice. Bring to a boil. Reduce the heat and steam for 20 minutes or until the water has completely evaporated.

Makes 4 servings.

KONGNAMUL BAB
RICE WITH YELLOW BEAN SPROUTS

On festive occasions and at parties, plain boiled rice is
always served. When other ingredients are added,
Koreans consider rice a "family dish." Rice with bean
sprouts provides a tasty example of such a filling supper
recipe.

2 cups rice   1 scallion
1 pound bean sprouts   1 clove garlic
¼ pound beef (flank,   1¾ cups water
   chuck or shoulder)

1. Wash the rice, then let it stand, covered, in 1¾ cups
water. Rinse the bean sprouts and remove any black ends.
Shred the beef into 2-inch lengths. Cut the scallion into
2-inch pieces, then shred lengthwise into very fine strips.
Crush the garlic. Add all these ingredients to the rice.

2. Bring the rice and the bean sprout mixture to a boil.
Simmer over a low flame for 20 minutes or until dry.

Makes 4 servings.

Sauce
1 scallion   1 teaspoon sesame seeds
1 clove garlic   1 teaspoon sesame oil
⅓ cup soy sauce

1. Mince the scallion and crush the garlic. Combine these ingredients with the soy sauce, sesame seeds and sesame oil in a bowl.

2. The sauce should be sprinkled lightly over the rice.

KIMCHI BAB
RICE WITH KIMCHI

When cooking rice with vegetables that tend to be
watery, use a little less than the 2 cups water usually
allotted for the rice. This particular blend of rice and
kimchi is definitely a "country-style" dish, to be used
when the budget is low or the cupboard bare.

2 cups rice	1 clove garlic
¼ pound pork	1 cup kimchi
1 scallion	1¾ cups water

1. Wash the rice, then let it stand covered in 1¾ cups
water. Shred the pork into 2-inch lengths. Cut the scallion
into 2-inch pieces, then shred lengthwise into very fine
strips. Crush the garlic. Add all these ingredients,
including 1 cup kimchi to the rice.

2. Bring the rice and kimchi mixture to a boil, then
simmer over a low flame for 20 minutes or until dry.

Makes 4 servings.

Variation: Use strips of beef instead of pork.

KONG BAB
RICE WITH BLACK BEANS

Kong Bab, no doubt because it is so economic, is the mainstay of the jailhouse. From this has evolved a popular saying, "Watch your step or you will eat Kong Bab." Kong Bab is, in fact, the slang expression for jail.

In Korea, a home which serves Kong Bab is in definite financial difficulties. However, you may wish to try a bit of culinary "slumming": the taste is an interesting variation on plain rice. The black beans dominate the rice with their flavor and color.

½ cup round black beans   2 cups water
½ cup rice

1. Quickly wash the black beans in cold water. Rinse the rice.

2. Bring the black beans to a boil in 2 cups water, then simmer for 20 minutes over a low flame. Add the rice and cook for 20 minutes longer or until dry.

Makes 4 servings.

Variation: For a more delicate taste, place a dozen black beans in 2 cups water and simmer for 20 minutes. Add slightly less than 2 cups rice and bring to a boil for a second time. Steam for 20 minutes or until dry.

PAT BAB
RICE WITH RED BEANS

Not to be confused with Kong Bab. Rice with red beans, Pat Bab, is definitely a festive dish.

½ cup round red beans   2 cups water
½ cup rice

1. Quickly wash the red beans in cold water. Rinse the rice.

2. Bring the red beans to a boil in 2 cups water, then simmer for 20 minutes over a low flame. Add the rice and cook for 20 more minutes or until dry.

Makes 4 servings.

Variation: For a less pronounced red bean taste, bring a dozen red beans to a boil in 2 cups water. Then simmer for 20 minutes. Add slightly less than 2 cups rice, boil a second time, then steam until dry.

OH KOK BAB
FIVE-GRAIN RICE

The numerous rich and heavy ingredients used in this rice
concoction definitely make it a party offering. In Korea
it is traditionally cooked on January 15th of the Lunar
calendar.

¼ cup black beans   ¼ cup red beans
¼ cup green beans   cold water

3½ cups water   1 cup millet
1½ cups Oriental
   rice cake

1. Place the black, green and red beans in separate pots
filled with water. Bring the water to a boil. Boil for
1 minute, then drain.

2. Combine the black, green and red beans in a large
saucepan. Cover the beans with 3½ cups cold water and
bring to a boil. Reduce the heat and simmer for 10
minutes.

3. Add the rice cake and millet. Boil a second time,
reduce the heat and let simmer for another 10 minutes or
until all the water has been absorbed.

Makes 6 servings.

SEASONINGS AND DECORATIONS

KANCHANG
SOY SAUCES

Soy sauce is one of the most popular condiments used in Korean cooking. For a more savory-tasting meat or vegetable, try the flavored soy sauce or vinegar soy sauce recipe.

Flavored Soy Sauce

2 tablespoons soy sauce
1 tablespoon beef broth

pinch sugar
drip sherry (optional)

1. Mix all ingredients in a bowl.

Vinegar Soy Sauce

2 tablespoons soy sauce
pinch sugar

1 tablespoon white vinegar

1. Mix all ingredients in a bowl.

Soy Sauce for Raw Fish

2 teaspoons wasabi powder
2 tablespoons soy sauce

1 tablespoon vinegar
pinch sugar

1. Mix the wasabi with water until it has the consistency of paste. Allow the mixture to stand, covered, for 5 minutes to attain full strength.

2. Add the soy sauce, vinegar and sugar to the mixture.

3. Slice thin a boned sea bass, then dip it into the sauce.

KOCHU CHANG
RED BEAN PASTE

Red bean paste is particularly tasty served with fresh scallions and radishes or added to some soups. Korean kochu chang may be purchased at many Oriental food stores. If it is not available, Japanese miso sauce may be substituted. This recipe is for a more pungent kochu chang than that which comes directly from the jar.

2 tablespoons red bean
   paste
2 tablespoons powdered
   red cayenne pepper

2 tablespoons soy sauce
1 teaspoon sugar

1. Mix all the ingredients well. Serve in a small dish for dipping.

JAT KOCHU CHANG
RED BEAN PASTE WITH PINE NUTS

This sauce can be used as a dip for fresh vegetables.

1 scallion
4 tablespoons pine nuts
2 tablespoons red bean
   paste

1 tablespoon sesame
   seeds

1. Mince the scallion and the pine nuts. Mix all the ingredients in a bowl and serve in a small dish.

KAE
SESAME SEEDS

A small supply of sesame seeds should be kept on hand if
any Korean cooking is planned. These seeds should
always be crushed and roasted.

1. Purchase a jar of white sesame seeds.

2. In a heavy skillet, *over a very low flame* brown the
seeds until they turn dark golden. Shake the pan and stir
the seeds from time to time. If the sesame seeds have
browned carefully, they will pop and jump in the pan.
Sesame seeds taste best when roasted to a dark
golden color.

3. Allow the seeds to cool to room temperature in the
pan. Crush them with a mortar and pestle or in a blender.
Crushed in either manner, the juice from the seeds will
escape. Stored in an air-tight jar, the seeds will
keep for months.

EGG DECORATION

Koreans often use strips of cooked egg to enhance the appearance of many dishes, including soups.

1 egg   ½ teaspoon oil or butter

1. Beat the egg well. Pour the egg into a large greased frying pan, forming a very thin layer. Cook the egg until almost done, then place under a broiler so that the top will be completely cooked. Remove the egg by turning the pan upside down.

2. Roll up the egg and cut crosswise into very thin strips for use as decoration.

Variation: Use 2 eggs and separate the whites from the yolks. Continue to cook separately to make both white and yellow decoration.

DESSERTS

BAM CHO
HONEYED CHESTNUTS

This is not a true dessert, but rather an after-dinner
taste treat.

1 cup dried chestnuts   3 cups water
½ cup honey

1. Simmer the chestnuts in 3 cups water for 30 minutes
or until they become soft, both inside and out. Drain the
chestnuts, reserve ½ cup water. Add honey to the
chestnuts and to this water and heat over a low flame.
Shake the pot in a circular movement until the honey has
melted. The melting will take about 5 minutes. (If the
chestnuts are touched, they will break apart.)

Makes 5 servings.

KUL DAECHU
HONEYED JUJUBES (RED DATES)

1 cup dried jujubes   ½ cup honey
1 tablespoon salt   ½ cup water
2 cups water

1. Wash the jujubes. Stir the salt into the water, then pour the solution over the jujubes and let stand overnight. Drain and throw away the salt water.

2. Combine the honey, ½ cup water and jujubes in a heavy pot. Simmer for 30 minutes.

Makes 5 servings.

SAENG KANG CHUNKWA
HONEYED GINGER

Honeyed ginger is a dessert for those who prefer the unusual tasting. Here is a treat that presents an interesting combination of the sweet and the hot. It has the further advantage of being good for the digestion. Serve either at room temperature or cold; it may be prepared well ahead of time.

½ pound raw ginger or 1 cup sliced	3½ cups water ½ cup honey

1. Peel the fresh ginger and slice thin on a diagonal. In an uncovered saucepan, boil the ginger in 3 cups water vigorously 10 minutes. Drain. (Do not discard this water, it may be used for ginger nectar. It cannot, however, be used for this recipe.)

2. Combine ½ cup water and honey with the ginger. Simmer over a low flame for 30 minutes, uncovered. There should be ½ cup concentrated liquid remaining in the saucepan.

YAK KWA

KOREAN CAKES (CHRYSANTHEMUM FLOWER CAKES)

These small cakes made with honey and wine are very
rich. In Korea, such cakes are often served at
special afternoon "tea parties."

2 tablespoons honey
2 tablespoons wine or
  sherry
2 tablespoons water
2 cups white flour

2 tablespoons sesame oil
1 cup water
1 cup honey
2 cups salad oil

1. Combine the honey, water and wine in a saucepan. Stir
over a very low flame for 5 minutes, remove from heat
and cool to room temperature.

2. Combine the honey, water and wine mixture with the
flour and sesame oil. Knead for 3 minutes. Roll out the
dough to ¾-inch thickness. Cut into chrysanthemum
shapes with a biscuit cutter.

3. Combine the remaining honey and water in saucepan.
Melt the honey over a low flame for 5 minutes. Cool
to room temperature.

4. Heat 2 cups oil to 400 degrees. Add the flower-shaped
pieces of dough one by one. Fry them until they float
to the top of the oil, which must remain very hot.

5. Remove the flower shapes from the hot oil and place them immediately into the honey-water mixture. Allow to stand for at least 24 hours. The longer the cakes stand, the better they taste. They harden and become crunchier as they absorb the honey.

Makes about 25 cakes.

INSAM CHUNKWA
GINSENG CAKE

Ginseng has been valued for centuries for its restorative and recuperative powers. Ginseng roots are expensive but are well worth their cost. A wise Korean wife will serve her husband ginseng as often as she can afford.

4 dried Korean ginseng roots	2 cups water
	½ cup honey

1. Simmer the ginseng roots in water for 4 hours in a heavy pot. There should be ½ cup liquid left after this time.

2. Add the honey and cook over an extremely low flame for 2 hours longer. Do not add more water for the ginseng will be ruined. If there is any risk of burning the ginseng, remove the pot from the stove after 1 hour. The ginseng roots should then be quite soft.

3. Cut the roots on a diagonal into thin slices.

Makes 4 servings.

YAK SIK
MEDICINAL CAKE

Requiring a great deal of time and effort to prepare, this delicious and exotic dessert provides a fitting climax to a holiday feast. The medicinal powers of this strangely-named rice cake remain unproved; but its power to generate a festive and convivial mood is unquestioned.

2 pounds Oriental rice cake (the small, round and tender variety)
7 cups water
30 dried chestnuts or ½ pound
3 cups hot water
20 jujubes (red dates)

⅓ cup black raisins
7⅓ tablespoons soy sauce
1 cup sugar
1 cup honey
8 cups water
⅓ cup sesame oil
5 cups water

1. Soak 2 pounds rice cake in 7 cups water overnight.

2. Bring the dried chestnuts to a boil in 3 cups hot water, Continue boiling for 45 minutes or until soft, but not falling apart. Rinse the chestnuts under cold water and remove any remaining skins. Set aside.

3. Bring the jujubes to a boil in plenty of water. Simmer for 10 minutes and allow them to soak for a few hours. Soak the raisins at the same time.

4. In a saucepan over a low flame, melt the sugar in the soy sauce. Add the honey and remove the mixture from the flame after 5 minutes. The honey should just melt, not cook.

5. Heat 8 cups water in a steamer. On top of the wire rack or plate, spread a dampened dish towel, preferably of thin cotton, but not terry cloth. Put the soaked rice on the towel. Make a well in the center so that the steam may flow through. Steam for 30 minutes.

6. Blend thoroughly the steamed rice, jujubes, chestnuts, soy sauce mixture and sesame oil in a large mixing bowl.

7. Bring 5 more cups water to a boil in the steamer. Return the rice mixture to the towel and wrap it tightly so that none of the flavor will be lost. Cover the steamer and steam for 1 hour. Test for doneness: the rice should be soft but not mushy.

8. Take the towel containing the rice out of the steamer. Allow the rice mixture to cool to room temperature. The cooled cake may be shaped as desired or as follows: roll a small quantity into cylinders using wax paper or Saran Wrap. To serve, cut slices across the cylinder.

Makes 20 servings.

DRINKS

SOONG NUNG
RICE WATER

Koreans believe that the most nutritious rice is that which sticks to the bottom of a pot after cooking. Ever resourceful, they use these grains of rice to make an after-dinner drink.

1. Add a few cups water to the grains of rice which adhere to the bottom of the rice pot. Bring quickly to a boil.

2. Serve hot at the end of the meal. It aids digestion.

BORI CHA
BARLEY TEA

Toasted barley resembles light-colored coffee beans. It
may be obtained in packages from Oriental food stores.
Toasted barley is made into a mild drink that accompanies
almost every Korean meal. Barley tea is served cool in
summer and is heated slightly in winter, as an aid
to digestion.

4 cups water   4 teaspoons toasted
                                              barley

1. Bring the water to a boil. Drop the barley into the
water and boil vigorously for 5 minutes. Strain and serve.

Makes 4 servings.

SOO CHUNKWA
GINGER DRINK

Ginger drink is intoxicating, but nonalcoholic. It is often
served on joyous occasions during the winter and
especially at New Year's. It will keep for a few days.

½ pound ginger   1 pound jar honey
10 cups cold water   pine nuts
¾ pound dried jujubes   cinnamon
4 cups hot water

1. Wash, but do not peel the ginger. Slice it paper-thin.
Place the ginger in a pot. Add 10 cups cold water. Bring to
a boil and cook for 2½ hours. Discard the ginger,
but reserve the water.

2. Wash the jujubes under cold running water. Place
them in 4 cups hot water and bring to a boil. Cook for 30
minutes. Cool.

3. Bring the ginger water to a boil and add the honey.
Boil vigorously 5 to 10 minutes or until the honey has
been completely absorbed into the water. Cool.

4. Place a jujube at the bottom of each glass. Add the
ginger water, top each glass with 2 pine nuts and
sprinkle with a pinch of powdered cinnamon.

Makes 6 to 8 glasses.

GLOSSARY

ABALONE is a delicately-flavored, light tan shellfish whose meat is very firm. It is commonly sold in cans of varying sizes. As with most fish, the longer it is cooked, the tougher it gets. Abalone becomes rubbery, as does squid.

BAMBOO SHOOTS are the tender sprouts of the bamboo, off-white in color and shaped somewhat like a flower bud. They are most often sold canned in this country and they come in several sizes packed in water. Their flesh is tender but firm. Slight cooking is required.

BEAN CURD (bean cake) is a 3 inch by 3 inch square cake of pressed soybeans with the texture of a custard pudding. It is soft, fragile and bland; requires very slight cooking (it takes on a curdled quality if boiled too long) and may be purchased in Chinese and Japanese grocery stores by the piece. Covered with water for storage purposes, it will keep a day or two in the refrigerator. Bean curd is extremely nutritious.

BEAN SPROUTS may be grown in a few days in your own kitchen by following the directions on a package of dried bean sprouts. These may be obtained from health food stores as well as Oriental grocery stores. Sprouted beans are, of course, more convenient to use and are generally sold in one-pound cellophane-wrapped packages. They should be washed before use and will keep only a day or two in the refrigerator. Another type of soybean sprout called yellow soybean sprout may be found in Chinese grocery stores. The buds on these sprouts are larger and the stems thicker than those on the regular sprouts. Their taste is also more pronounced and their texture firmer.

BLACK BEANS are small and round. They are sold either by weight or in one-pound packages in Oriental grocery stores.

BLACK DRIED MUSHROOMS (Chinese mushrooms) have a black and brown striated skin and a distinctive flavor, unlike many other mushrooms. Sold dried by weight or in packages in Oriental grocery stores, they must be soaked for 30 minutes before use. Expanding considerably in size, they have a stem in the center which may remain the hardest part of the mushroom.

BUTTON MUSHROOMS are commonly found in most American grocery stores and supermarkets.

CHINESE CABBAGE is a green leafy vegetable with a long white stem, resembling a cross between lettuce and cabbage. Its flavor is much more subtle than that of the American cabbage. Perhaps the most widely used vegetable in Korean cooking, it can be found in Oriental food stores and is stocked by many greengrocers (usually Italian) who carry a wide variety of good vegetables.

CHINESE CHIVES are a cross between green onions (scallions) and chives. Their stems are dark green and flat rather than rolled as are our chives. Their flavor is not overbearing.

CHINESE TURNIPS are long white vegetables with almost no skin. They are widely used in Korea and may be found at the fresh vegetable corner of most Oriental grocery stores. They are sold by weight; the heavier pieces are better than the lighter ones of comparable size. These turnips are often called Chinese radishes, but because they are often a foot long it seems more appropriate to call them turnips. Their taste is subtle; their texture crisp and moist.

CLOUD-EAR MUSHROOMS (fungus) are thin, soft, dried mushrooms, sold by weight or in packages in Oriental grocery stores. When dry they look black, but after soaking they expand greatly and take on a brownish tinge. Cloud-ear mushrooms may be used in any recipe calling for mushrooms.

DAENCHANG (brown bean paste) is a muddy brown paste made from a mixture of soybeans and rice. It is hot-tasting, but like kochu chang, Its flavor is distinctive. Sold in jars, this paste is kept in the refrigerated department of Oriental grocery stores.

DRIED CHESTNUTS are shelled and sold by weight in Oriental food stores and in specialty stores.

DRIED CUTTLEFISH when whole is broad and flat, with remnants which look like feelers near the head. This fish can be eaten by peeling off the thin outer skin or can be used in soups. It is sold either whole or packaged in strips for nibbling.

DRIED SEAWEED (purple laver) is cultivated with particular care in Korea and is thought to be the best laver available. It is sold in packages of several sheets, paper-thin and folded in half.

DRIED GREEN SEAWEED is available in long strips about 1 inch wide. Korean seaweed is of superior quality, but is difficult to find. It is sold packaged in some Oriental grocery stores and must be washed and soaked before use. This seaweed expands considerably in size and you will find that a little goes a long way.

DRIED SQUID is a brown dried fish with a powdery-white coating. It is packaged whole and in pieces and is sold in Oriental grocery stores. It must be soaked before it is cooked or it may be chewed raw.

DUMPLING SKINS are squares of rolled dough. They may be found wrapped in plastic at the refrigerated section of Oriental grocery stores. These skins will keep in a freezer for several months.

GINGER ROOT when fresh has a thin, light-brown skin and a yellow interior with a potatolike texture. It comes in varying shapes, from nutlike rounds to large bunches in an antlerlike formation. When strictly fresh it cuts easily; the older it gets the more woody it becomes. Fresh ginger is quite pungent. It may be found in most well-stocked greengrocers (Italian, Puerto-Rican) and in all the Oriental grocery stores. It is also sold dried and powdered in most supermarkets.

GINGKO NUTS are small light brown nuts of the gingko tree. They are sold dried by weight and in cans.

GINSENG ROOT is used mostly for medicinal purposes and is highly prized for its rejuvenating qualities. It is usually sold dried in packaged form in Oriental stores.

GREEN BEANS are small and round. They are sold by weight or in one-pound packages in Oriental grocery stores.

JUJUBES (red dates) are used in sweet dishes; they are unlike our dates, but are similar in appearance to red prunes or dried plums. Sold by weight in Oriental grocery stores, they must be soaked before using.

KAT is a green vegetable which looks like a cross between celery and spinach. It may be bought in Oriental grocery stores.

KOCHU CHANG (red bean paste) is a dark reddish paste made from soybeans, rice and red pepper. It is a little spicy but not outrageously so. Sold in jars, this paste can be found at the refrigerated department of Oriental grocery stores. It will keep in the refrigerator for several months.

LOTUS ROOT (water lily root) resembles an overgrown sweet potato with brownish skin. When the root is sliced, eight or nine empty tubes which run lengthwise are revealed. It is sold in Oriental grocery stores fresh or canned.

MINIATURE SHRIMP are tiny bits of gloop unrecognizable as shrimp. Sold in bottles at the refrigerated counter of Oriental grocery stores, they are sometimes used in making kimchi.

MUNG PEAS are the small round greenish beans from which bean sprouts grow. (See bean sprouts.)

ORIENTAL RICE CAKE is smaller and rounder than other kinds of rice and when cooked, has a much softer consistency. It is sold in Oriental grocery stores.

PINE NUTS (pinon) are the nut-like edible seeds of the piñon tree and are used for decorative purposes.

RED BEANS are small and round. They are sold by weight or in one-pound packages in Oriental grocery stores. These beans are widely used in Korea for "sweet" confections.

RED PEPPER is ground into a powder and sold by weight in Oriental stores. Red cayenne pepper is similar and may be found in any supermarket. There are also red pepper flakes, which may be bought in supermarkets, in Italian grocery stores and in Oriental grocery stores. Whole fresh red peppers are carried by Italian and other well-stocked greengrocers. They are all, of course, hot, but some brands are hotter than others, depending on the original peppers and their age.

RICE FLOUR is a refined white flour milled from rice. It is sold packaged in boxes in Oriental grocery stores.

SEA CUCUMBER (bêche-de-mer, sea slug, trepang) is a mollusk found on coral reefs in the Pacific and considered a great delicacy in the Far East. Measuring about 6 inches long and sold dried in Oriental stores, it is either black or dark brown in color with prickles on its skin. Sea cucumber must be scrubbed, soaked and cooked for some time; then it becomes quite soft.

SESAME OIL is pressed from sesame seeds. It is a rather dark honey color and is heavier than salad oil. American sesame oil may be found in health food stores and specialty shops, but it is not at all comparable to a good Chinese or Japanese brand. It is much lighter and does not have the same strong flavor.

SESAME SEEDS are tiny white (or black) seeds sold packaged or by weight in Oriental grocery stores. They are also sold in jars in health food stores and in specialty shops. Sesame seeds which are purchased in small spice jars in supermarkets are expensive. American sesame seeds are just as good as those sold under Oriental brand names. They are extensively used for flavoring Korean dishes.

SHARK'S FINS resemble honey-colored, hairlike noodles —not at all what you would expect of a shark. They are sold only in Chinese grocery stores and are considered a fine but expensive delicacy. However, a little goes a long way and they will keep indefinitely.

SOY SAUCE is a brownish-black salty liquid made from fermented soybeans. It may replace salt in cooking. This sauce is extensively used in Korean dishes, giving them their distinct flavor. There are several kinds available: light, medium and heavy soy sauces are produced by the Chinese, and a medium soy sauce sold under the brand name Kikkoman is made by the Japanese. But the American variety which is marketed under a pseudo-Chinese name should never be used as a substitute for an imported soy sauce except in dire desperation.

SWEET RICE FLOUR (glutinous rice flour) is a refined white flour made from glutinous rice. It is sold packaged in boxes in Oriental grocery stores.

TRANSPARENT NOODLES (pea starch, cellophane noodles, shining noodles or vermicelli) are made from mung peas. These curious-looking noodles are white when dry and are sold in packages of varying weights. Dried in extremely long strips which all stick together, it is hard to pull them apart. They should be soaked in warm water before use and cooked very slightly because of their thinness. When cooked, they become opaque and slippery.

WASABI is a green powder resembling dried mustard in texture. It can be purchased at Oriental food stores.

INDEX

Cod, salt, with chicken and turnip; 156
Conchs, 163
Crabs, blue, 139; in soy sauce, 140
Cucumber, with pork, 201
Cucumber kimchi, 245-46
Cucumber vegetable, 174

Dates, red, honeyed, 270
Deep fried beef strips, 109; chicken strips, 126; pork strips, 118
Desserts:
  Ginseng cake, 274
  Honeyed chestnuts, 269
  Honeyed jujubes, 270
  Honeyed ginger, 271
  Korean cakes, 272-73

Egg decoration, 266
Eggplant, pork-stuffed, 203-204; stuffed, 191-92
Eggs:
  Beef omelet, 96-97
  Omelet with chives, 193-94
  Shrimp omelet, 133

Fish fried in egg batter, 145-46
Fish sauté, 144
Five-grain rice, 258

Ginger, honeyed, 271
Ginger drink, 281
Ginseng cake, 274
Green bean soup, 79
Green pepper quarters, stuffed, 199-200
Green peppers, with pork, 205; stuffed, 187-88
Grilled chicken in red sauce, 124; with soy sauce, 123
Grilled sole in red sauce, 155

Hamburger, Korean, 93-94; grilled, 95
Happiness pot, with beef, 226-27; with shell fish, 228-30; sauce, 225

Honeyed chestnuts, 269
Honeyed ginger, 271
Honeyed jujubes (red dates), 270

Instant kimchi, 235

Jujubes (red dates), honeyed, 270

Kidney, veal, 127
Kimchi:
  Casual, 238-39
  Cucumber, 245-46
  Instant, 235
  Quick, 240-41
  with rice, 255
  Stuffed, 243-44
  Substitute, turnip salad, 236
  Turnip-water, 237
  Water, 242
Korean cakes, 272-73

Laver, thin (seaweed), 169
Liver sautéed in egg batter, 128
Lobster, 141
Lobster soup, 53
Lotus roots, 231

Mackerel stew, 158-59
Meat, see Beef, Chicken, Pork, Veal
Meat, raw, 111 (See also *Beef:* Raw)
Meat sauce for vegetables, 179
Meatballs in sauce, 104-106
Medicinal cake, 275-76
Mussel and bean curd soup, 59

Nine–course hors d'oeuvre tray, 216–19; sauce, 215

Omelets:
  Beef, 96-97
  with chives, 193-94
  Shrimp, 133
Onion rings, with beef, 196-97
Onion soup with brown sauce, 68
Oxtail and beef soup stock, 47

INDEX OF KOREAN RECIPE TITLES

293